God Loves

_____

(Your name)

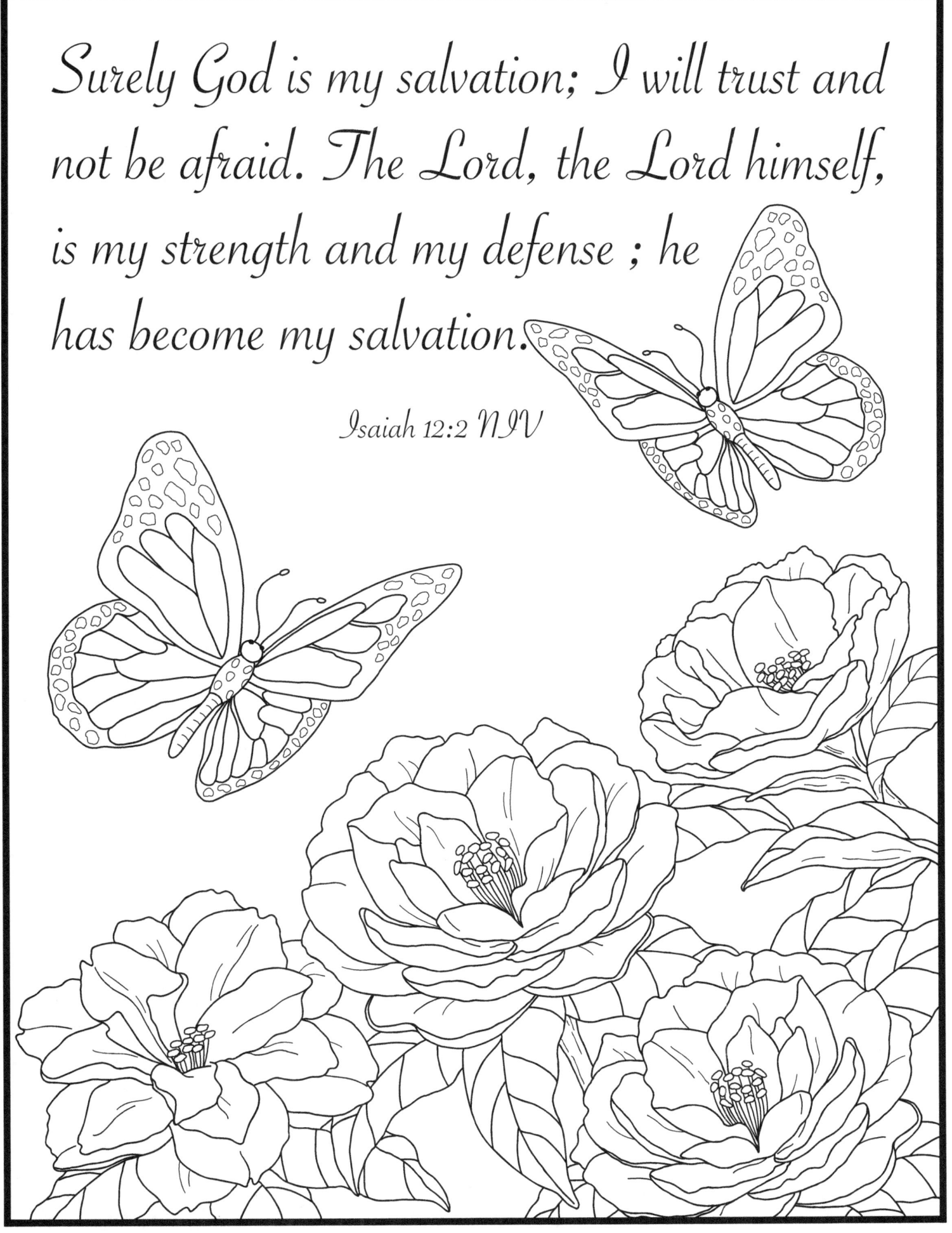

Trust in God for He is my salvation.

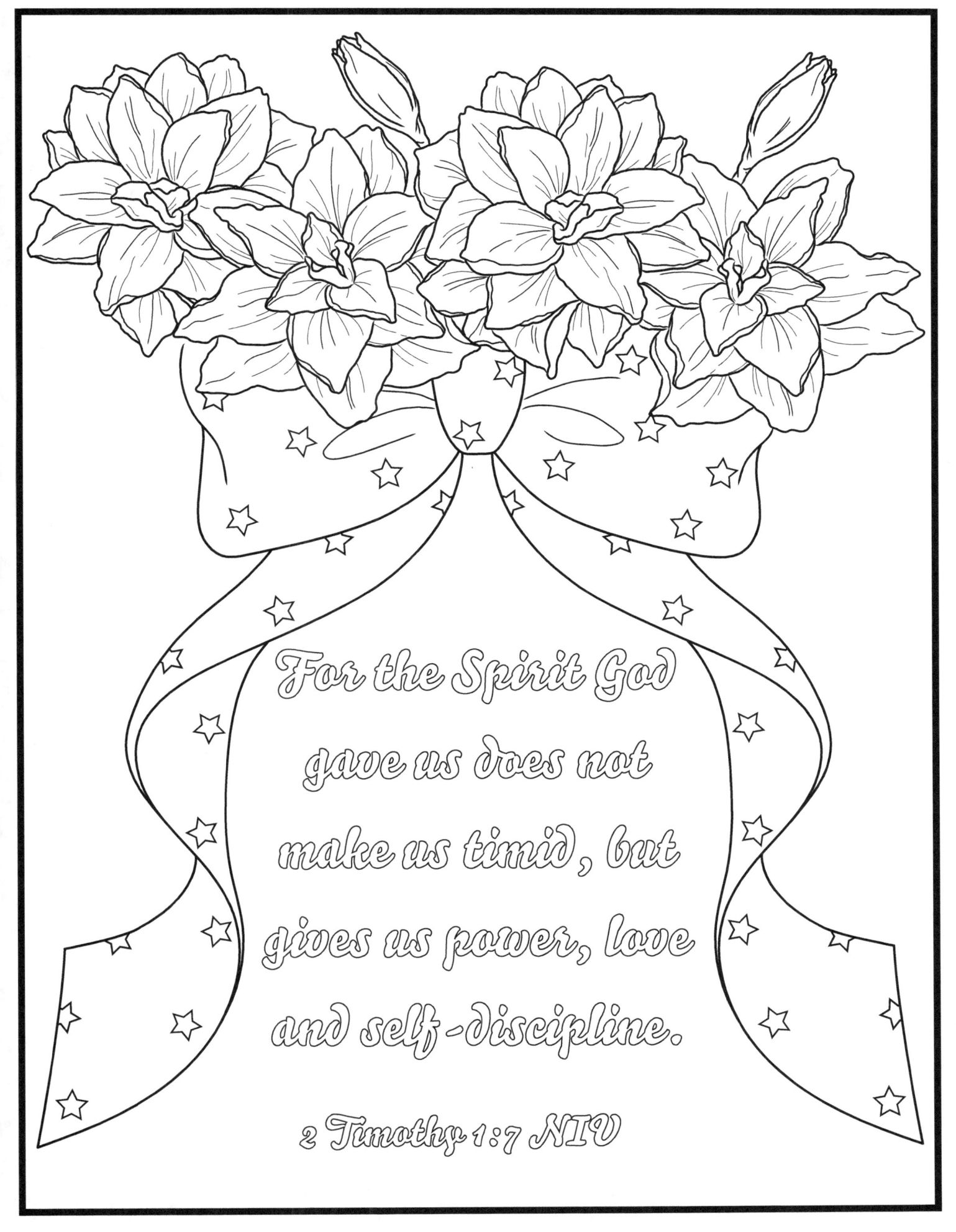

For the Spirit God gave us does not make us timid, but gives us power, love and self-discipline.

2 Timothy 1:7 NIV

Trust in God, He is with you.

Trust in God, He is with you.

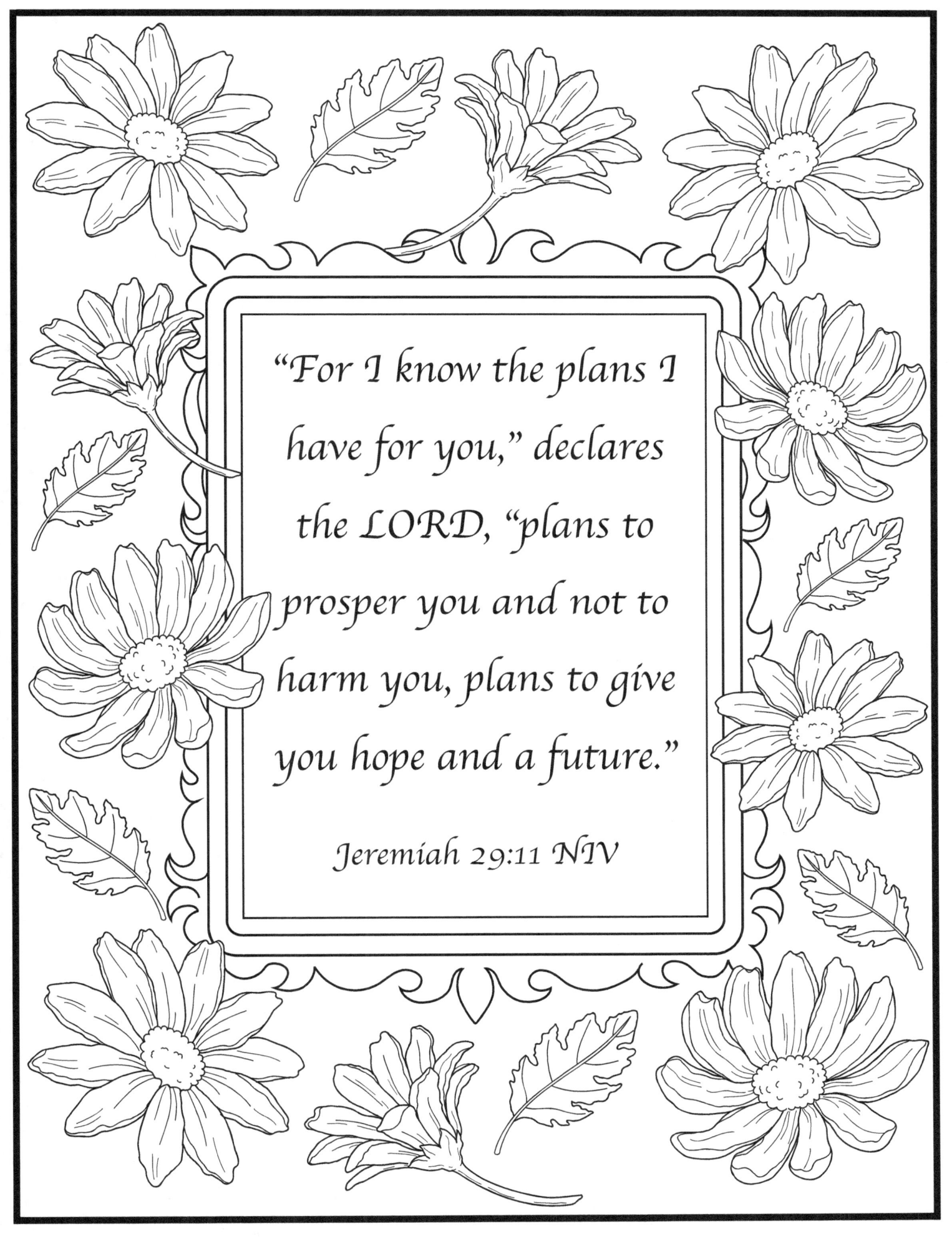

Trust in God, He comforts you in all your troubles.

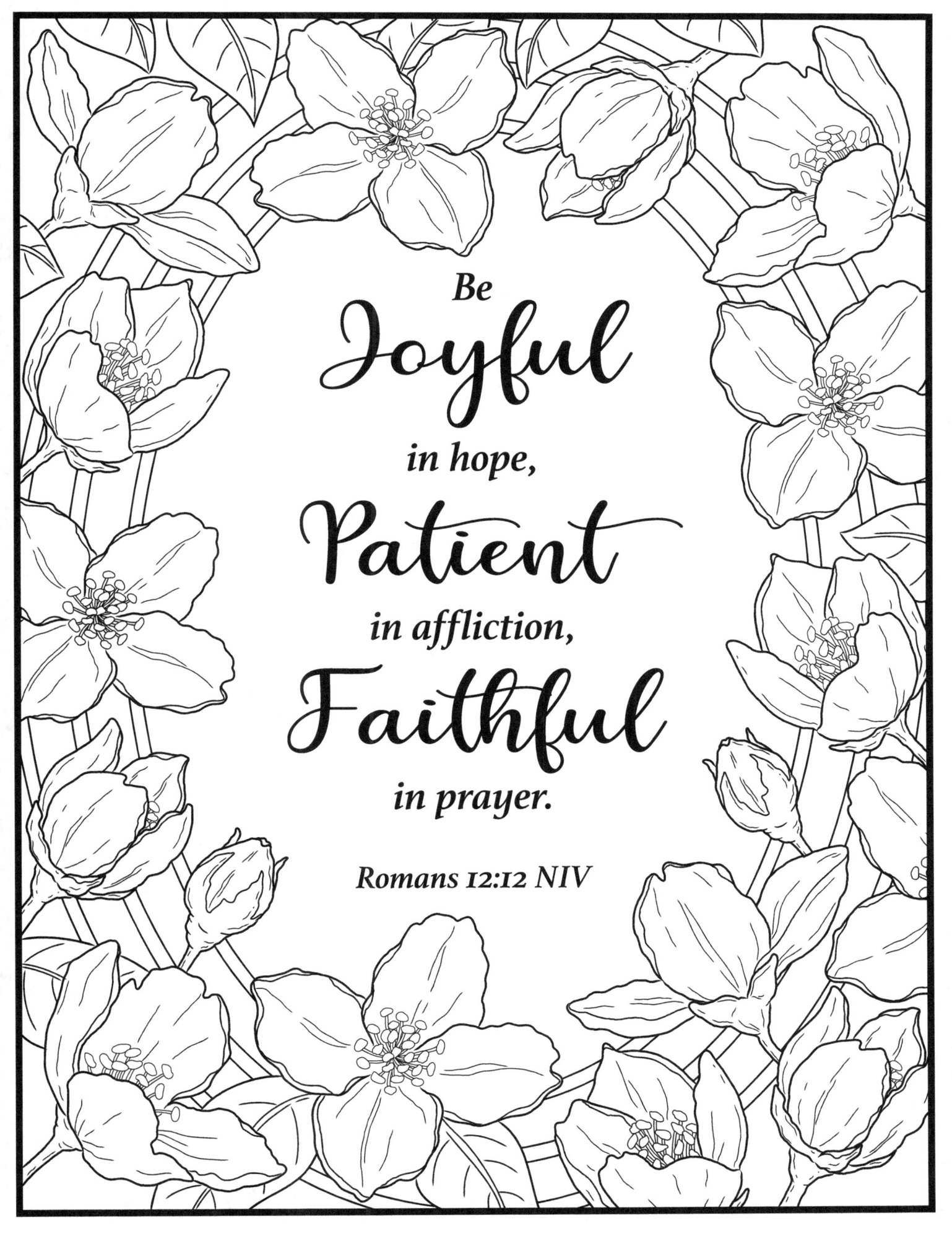

Trust in God, He has wonderful plans for you.

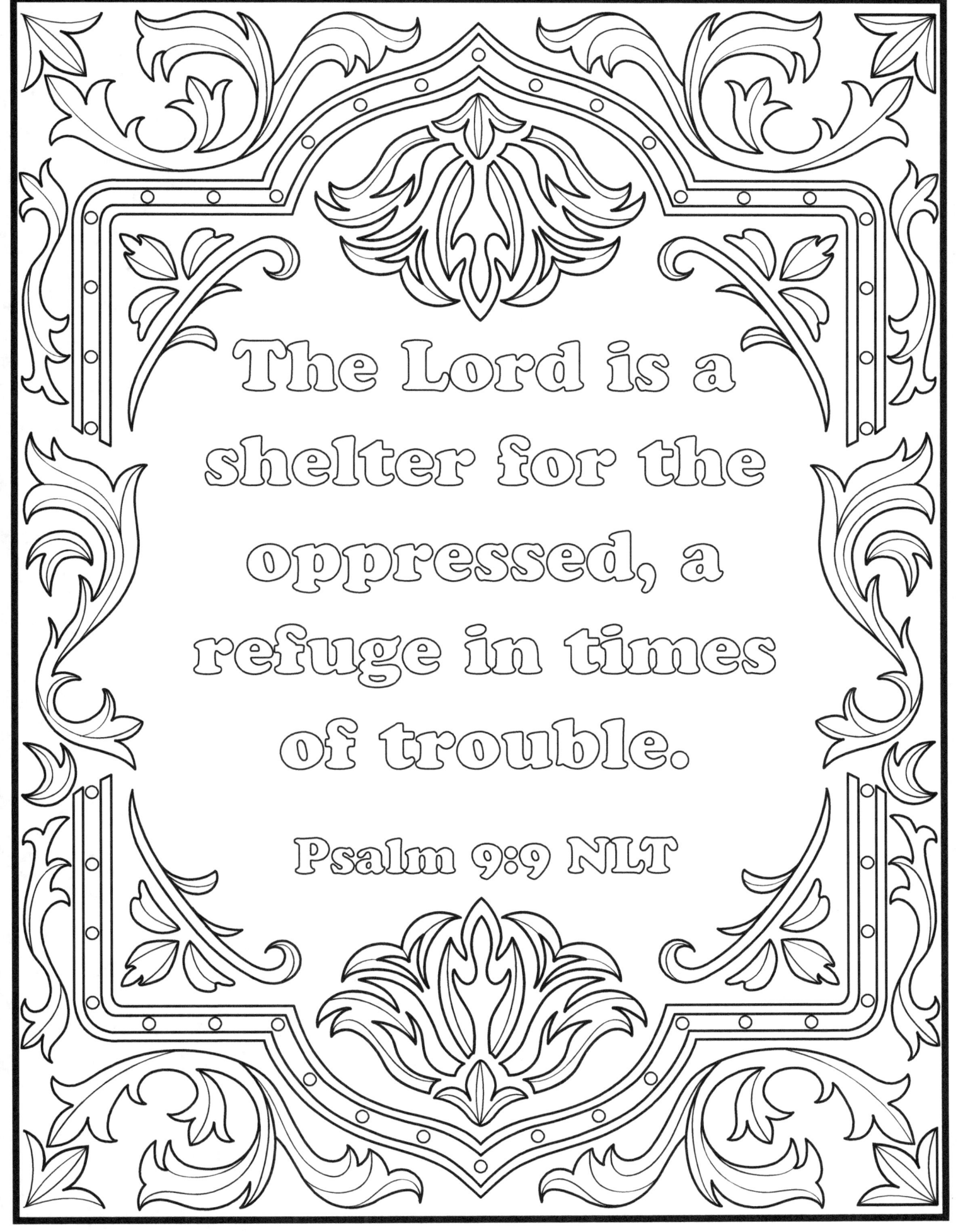

Trust in God, and fear not!

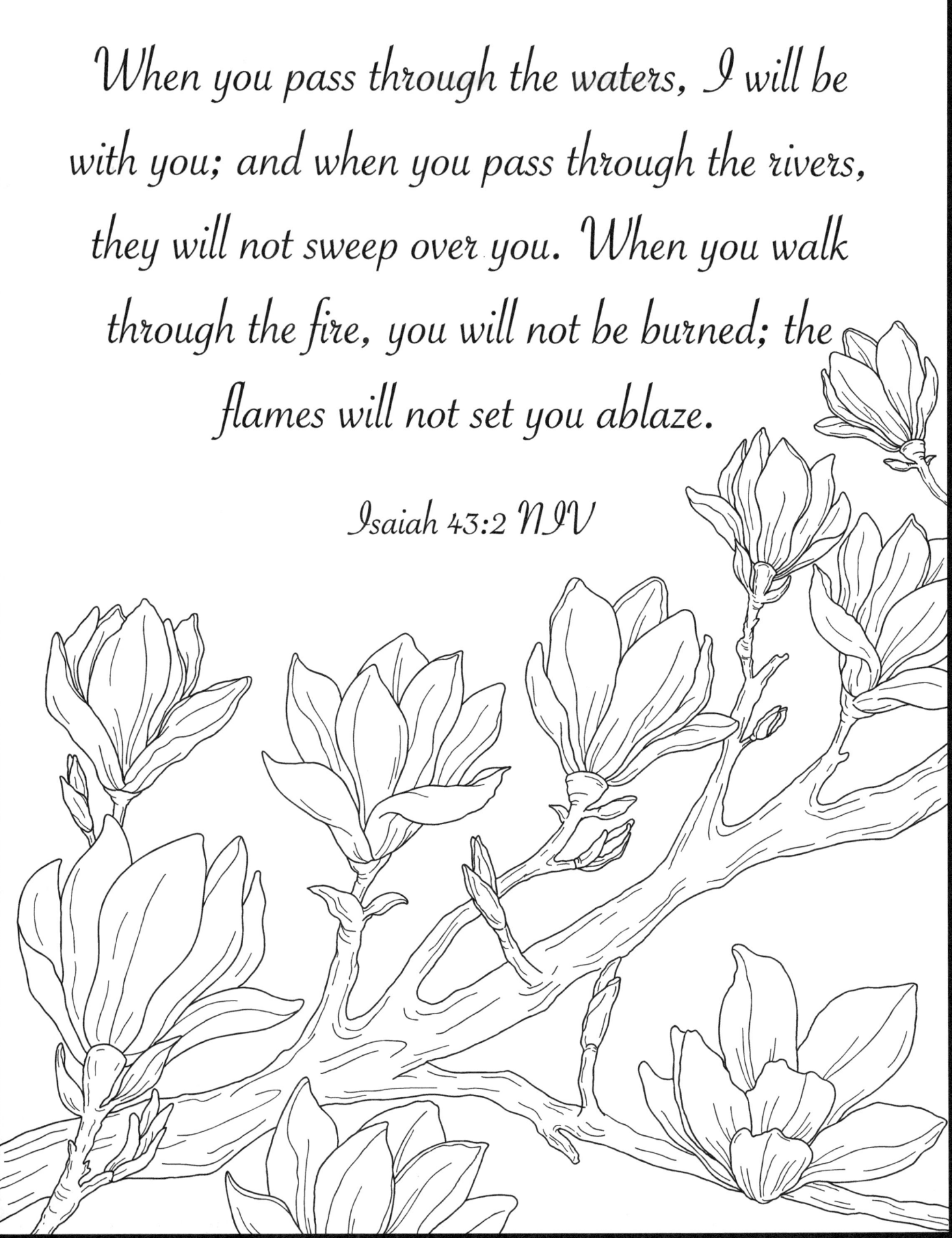

When you pass through the waters, I will be with you; and when you pass through the rivers, they will not sweep over you. When you walk through the fire, you will not be burned; the flames will not set you ablaze.

Isaiah 43:2 NIV

Trust in God, He is the light in your darkness.

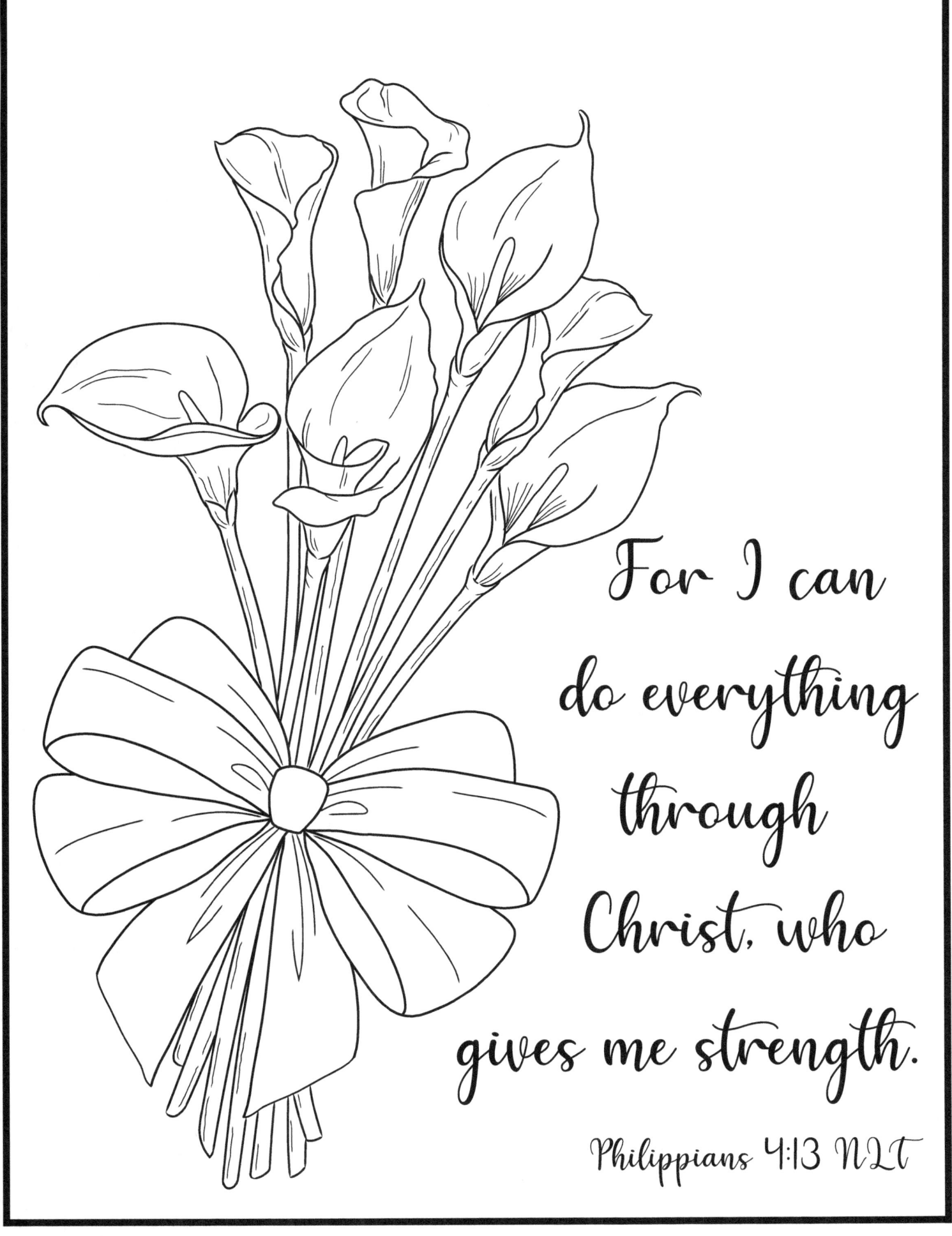

Trust in God, He will give you strength.

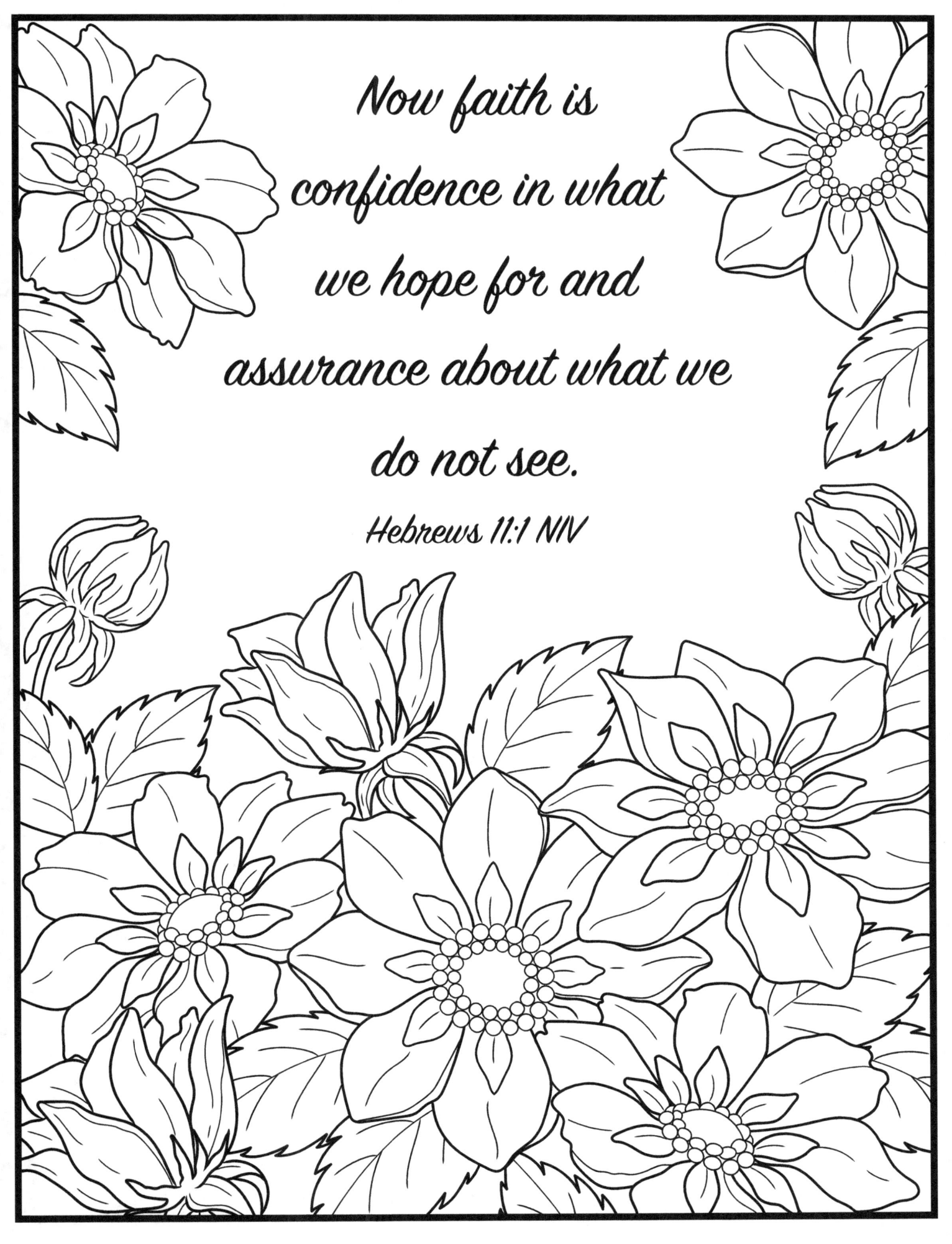

Trust in God, He is your hope.

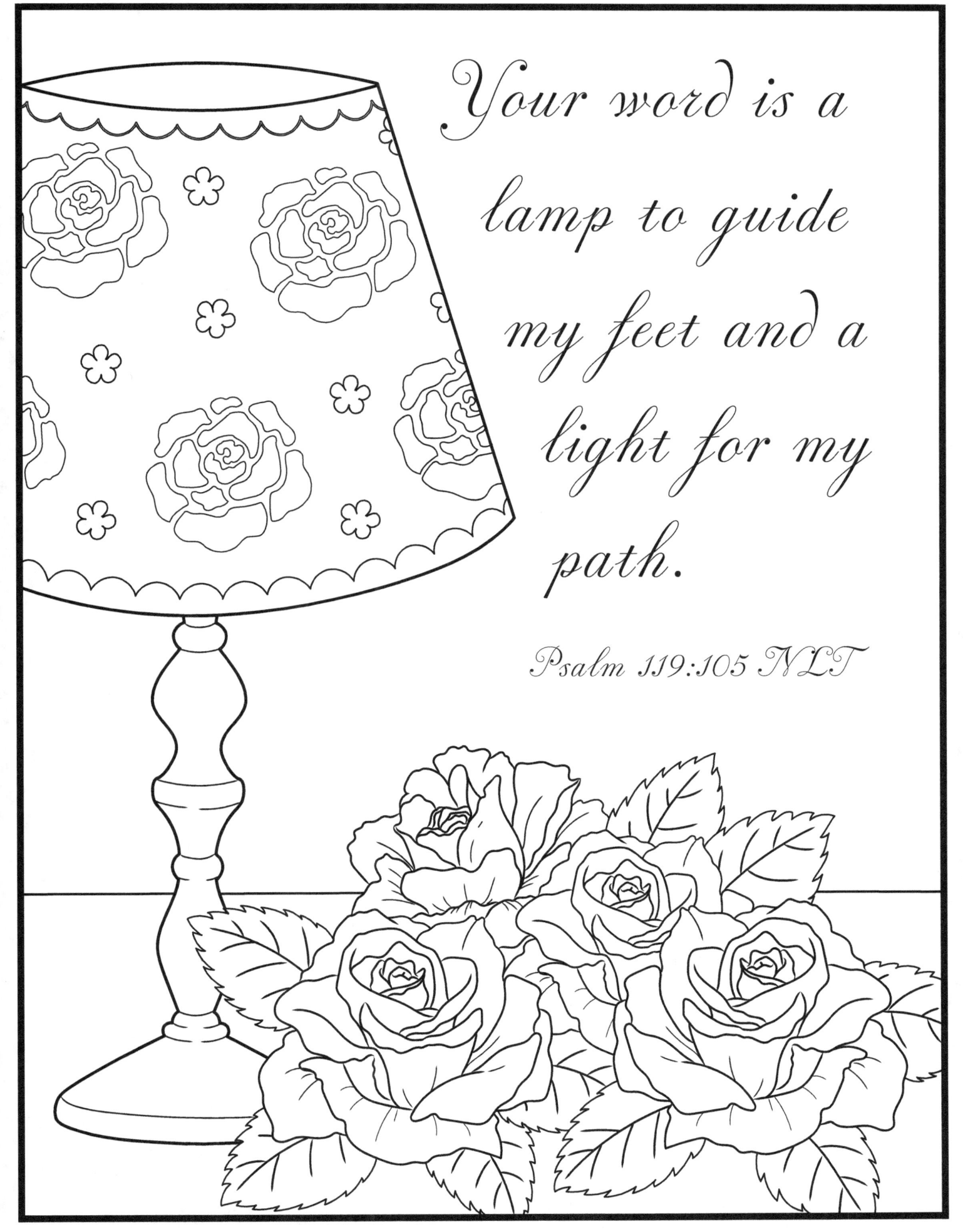

Your word is a lamp to guide my feet and a light for my path.

Psalm 119:105 NLT

Trust in God, He will guide you.

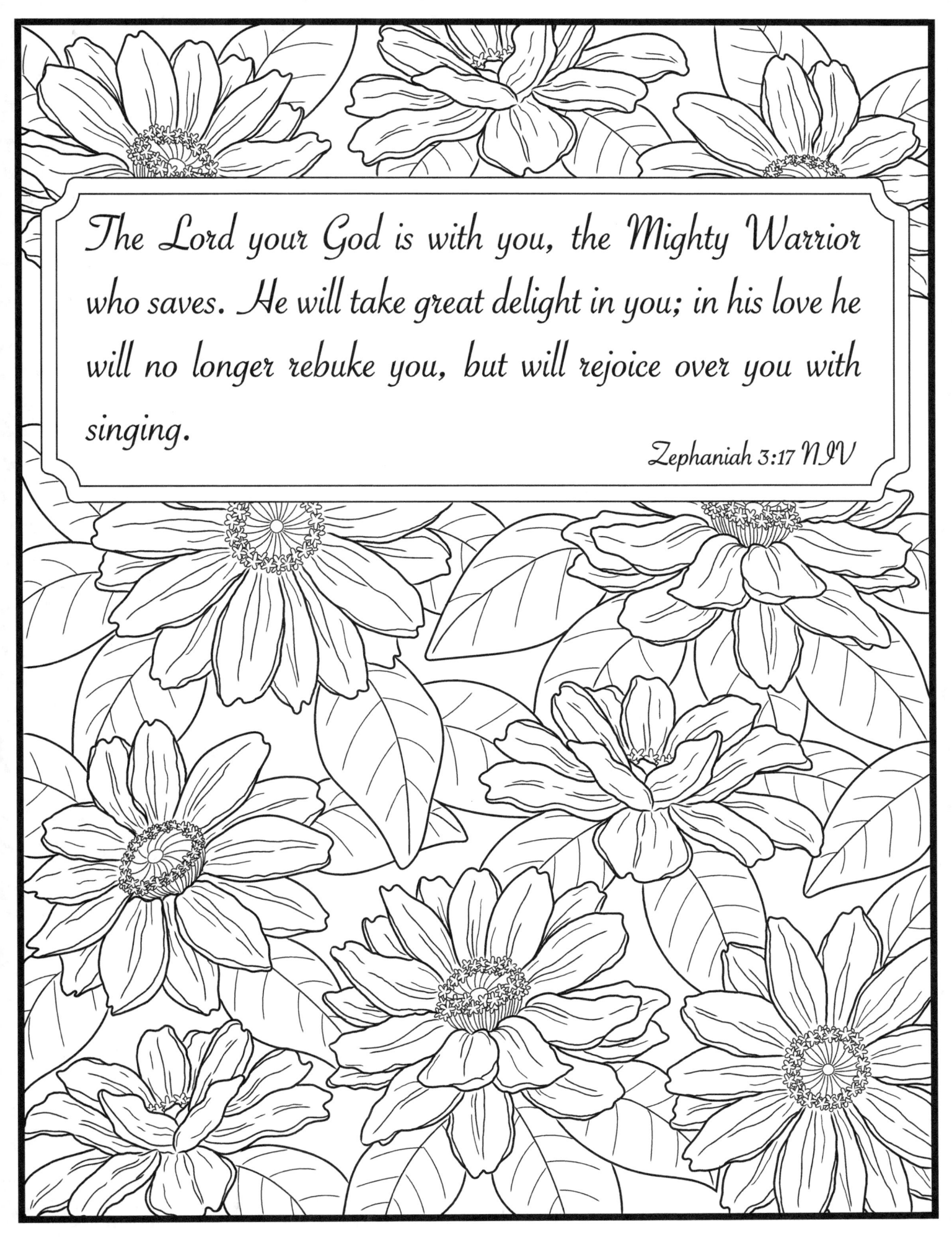

The Lord your God is with you, the Mighty Warrior who saves. He will take great delight in you; in his love he will no longer rebuke you, but will rejoice over you with singing.

Zephaniah 3:17 NIV

Trust in God, He will help you when you are in trouble.

May God our Father and the Lord Jesus Christ give you grace and peace.

1 Corinthians 1:3 NLT

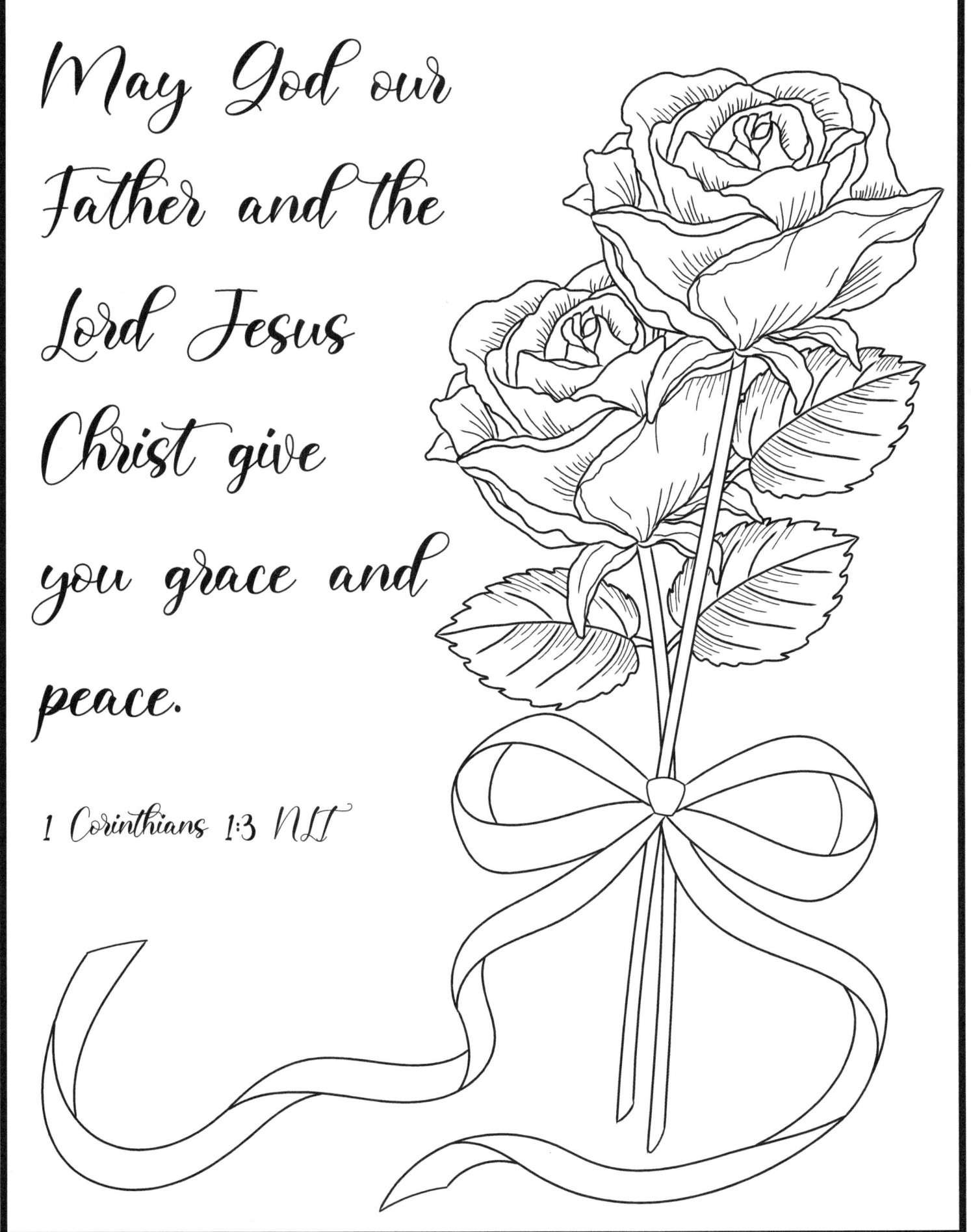

Trust in God, He will give you peace.

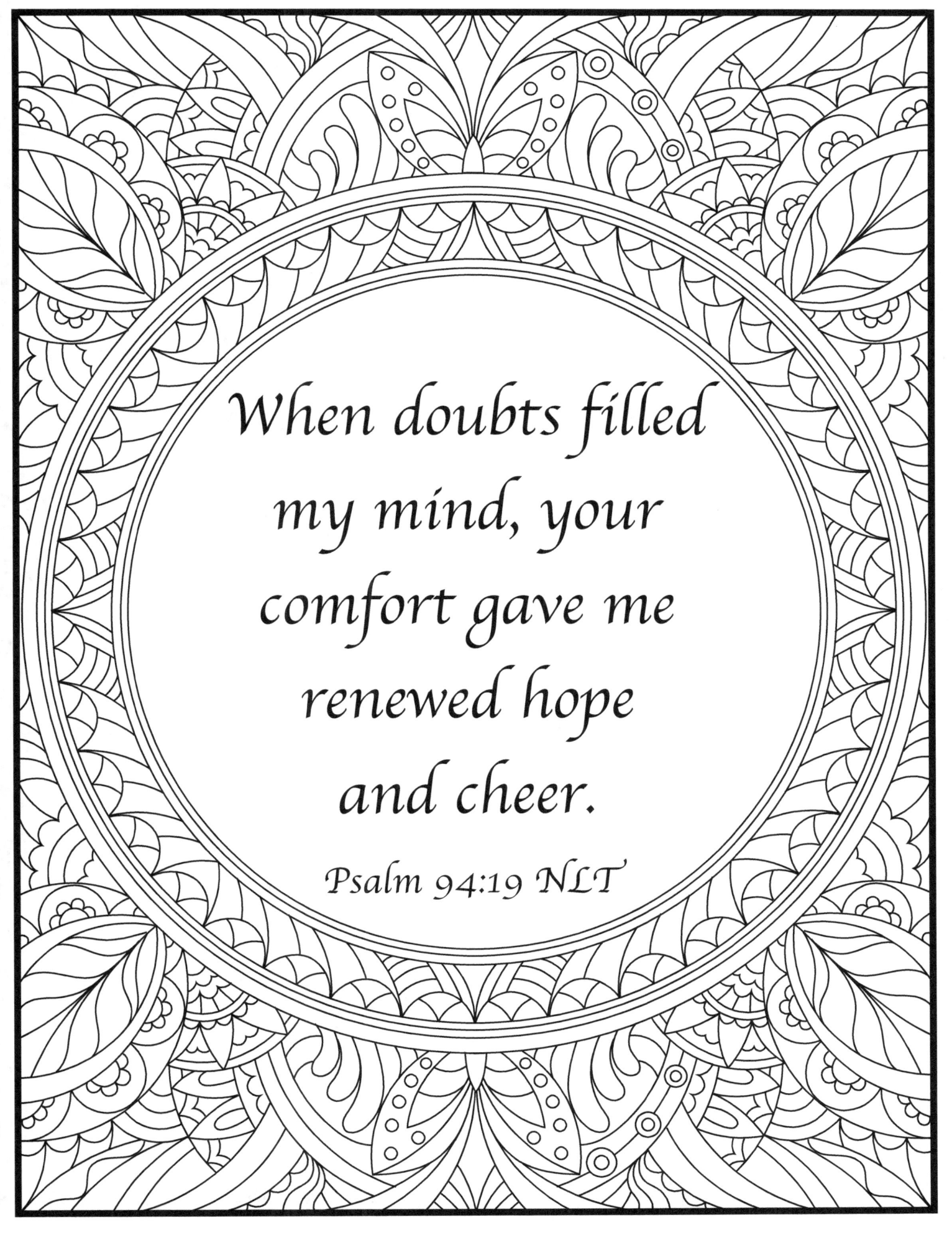

When doubts filled
my mind, your
comfort gave me
renewed hope
and cheer.

Psalm 94:19 NLT

Trust in God, He will help you overcome.

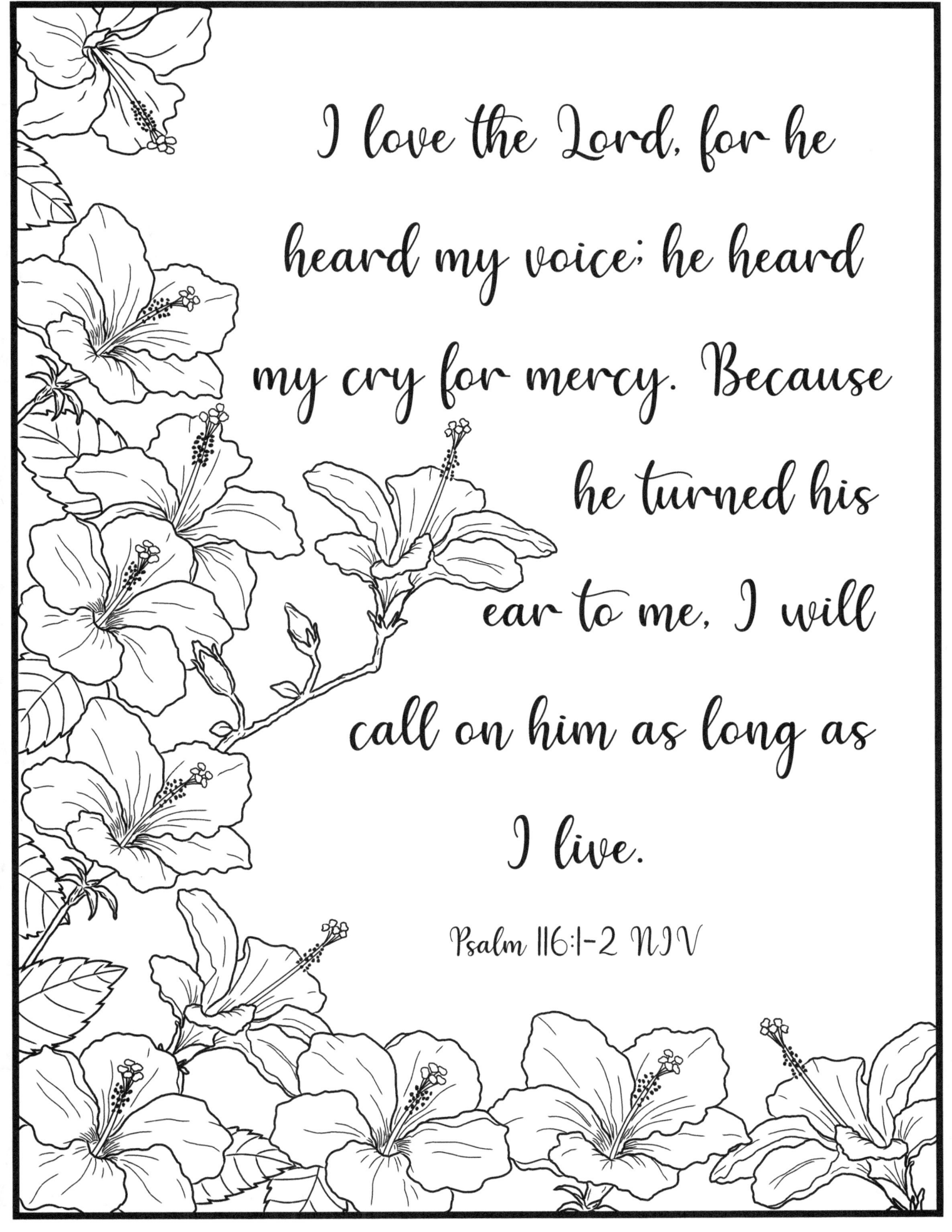

Trust in God, He will save you.

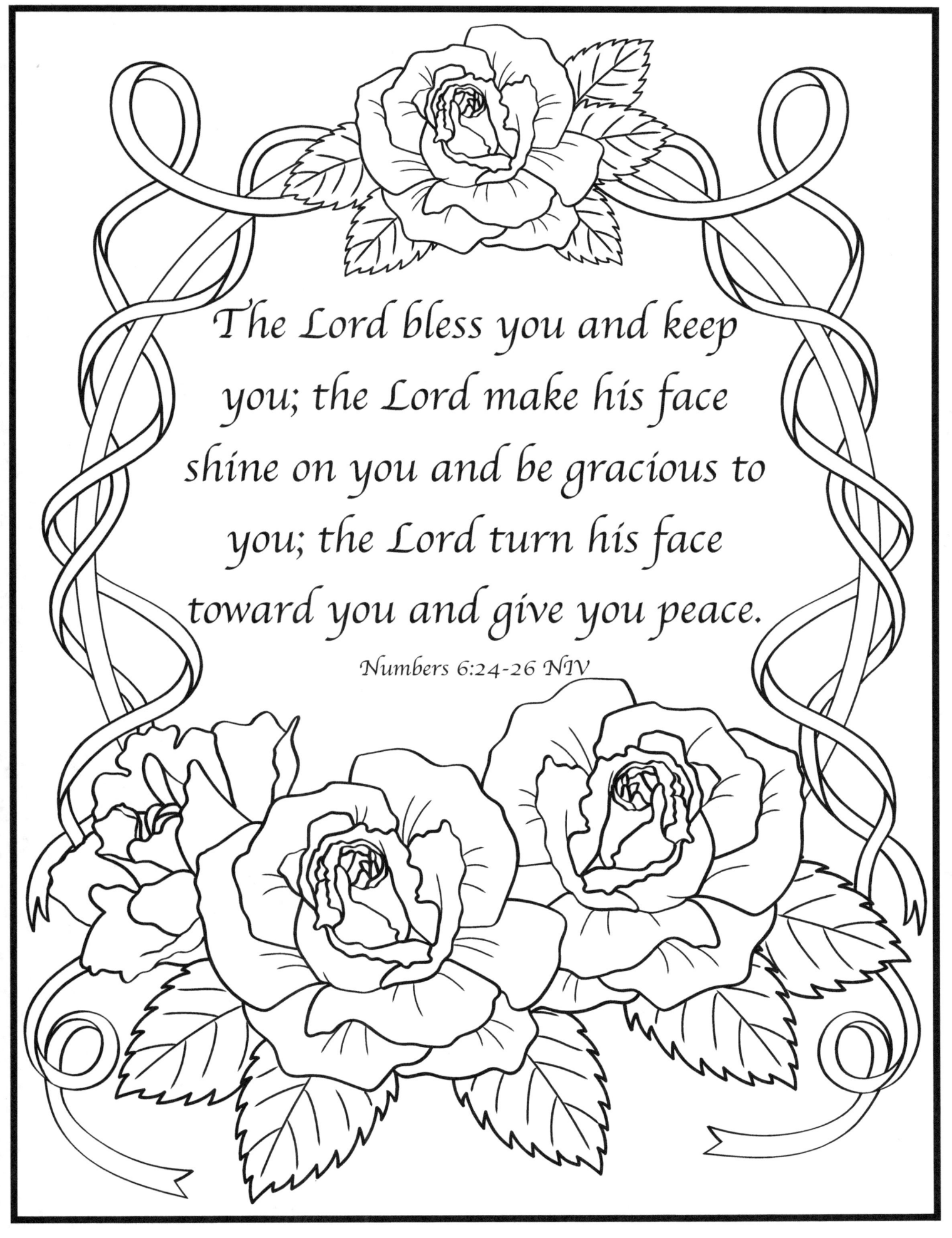

The Lord bless you and keep you; the Lord make his face shine on you and be gracious to you; the Lord turn his face toward you and give you peace.

Numbers 6:24-26 NIV

Trust in God, He will bless you.

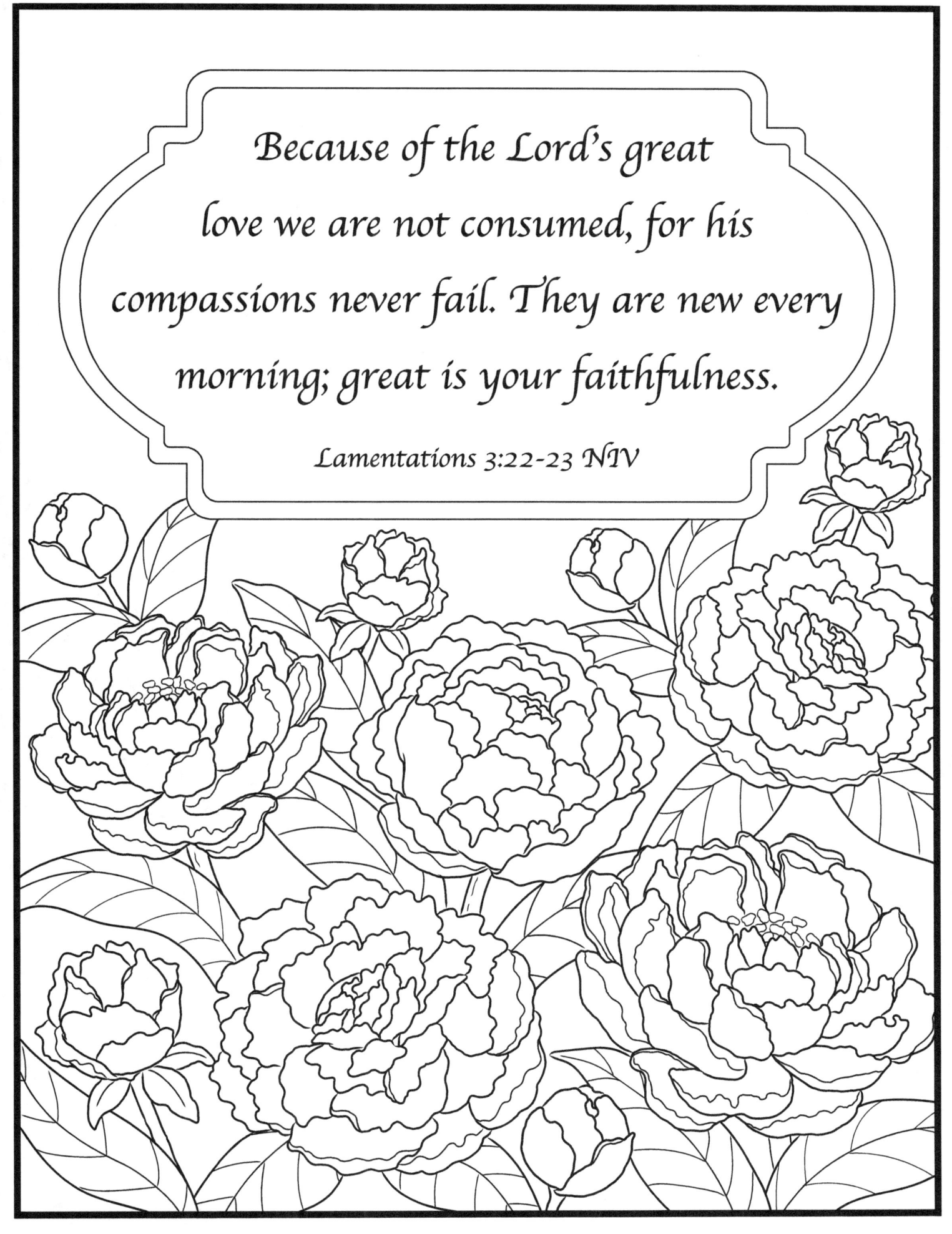

Because of the Lord's great love we are not consumed, for his compassions never fail. They are new every morning; great is your faithfulness.

Lamentations 3:22-23 NIV

Trust in God, He will show you mercy.

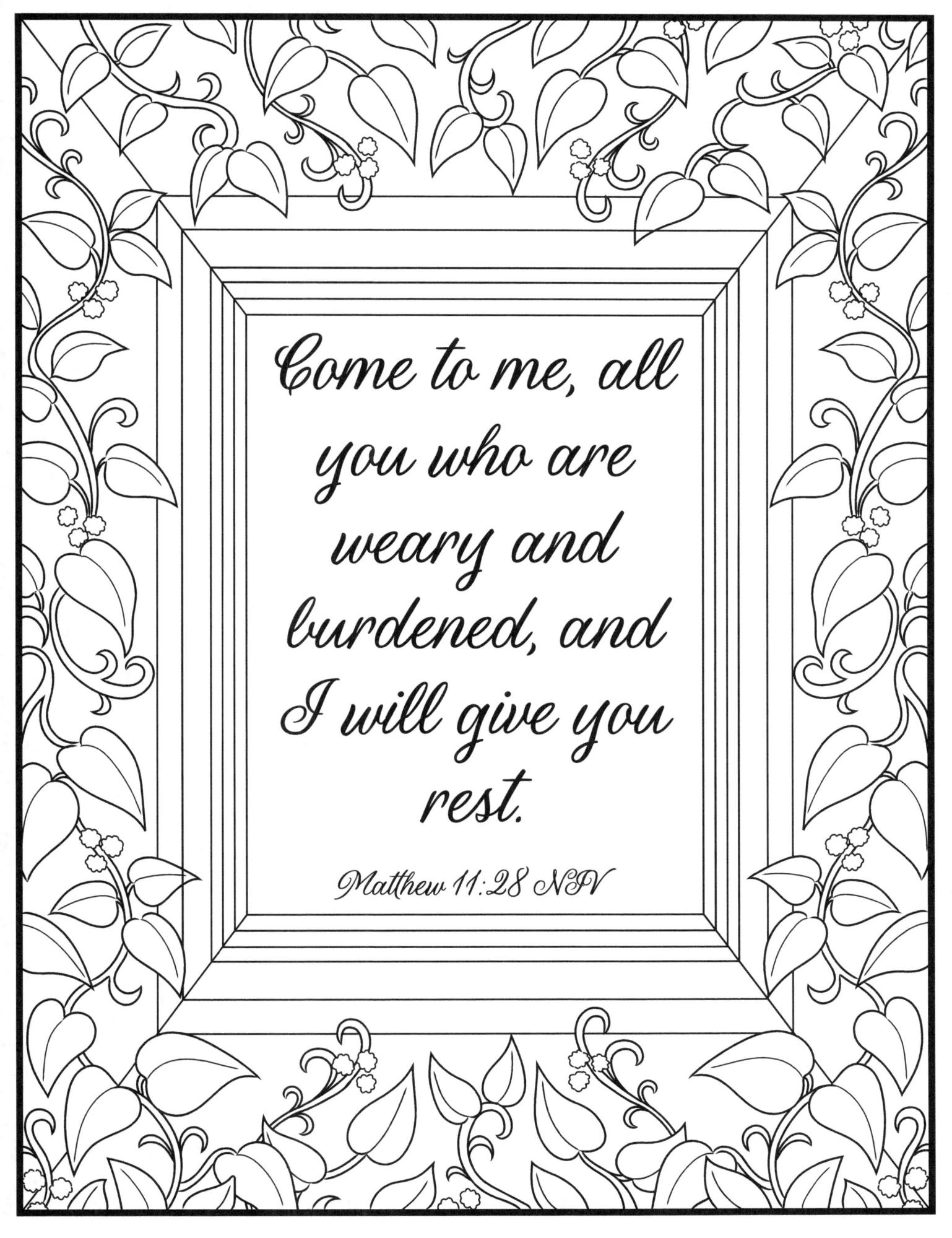

Come to me, all you who are weary and burdened, and I will give you rest.

Matthew 11:28 NIV

Trust in God, He will give you rest.

Trust in God, He will give you rest.

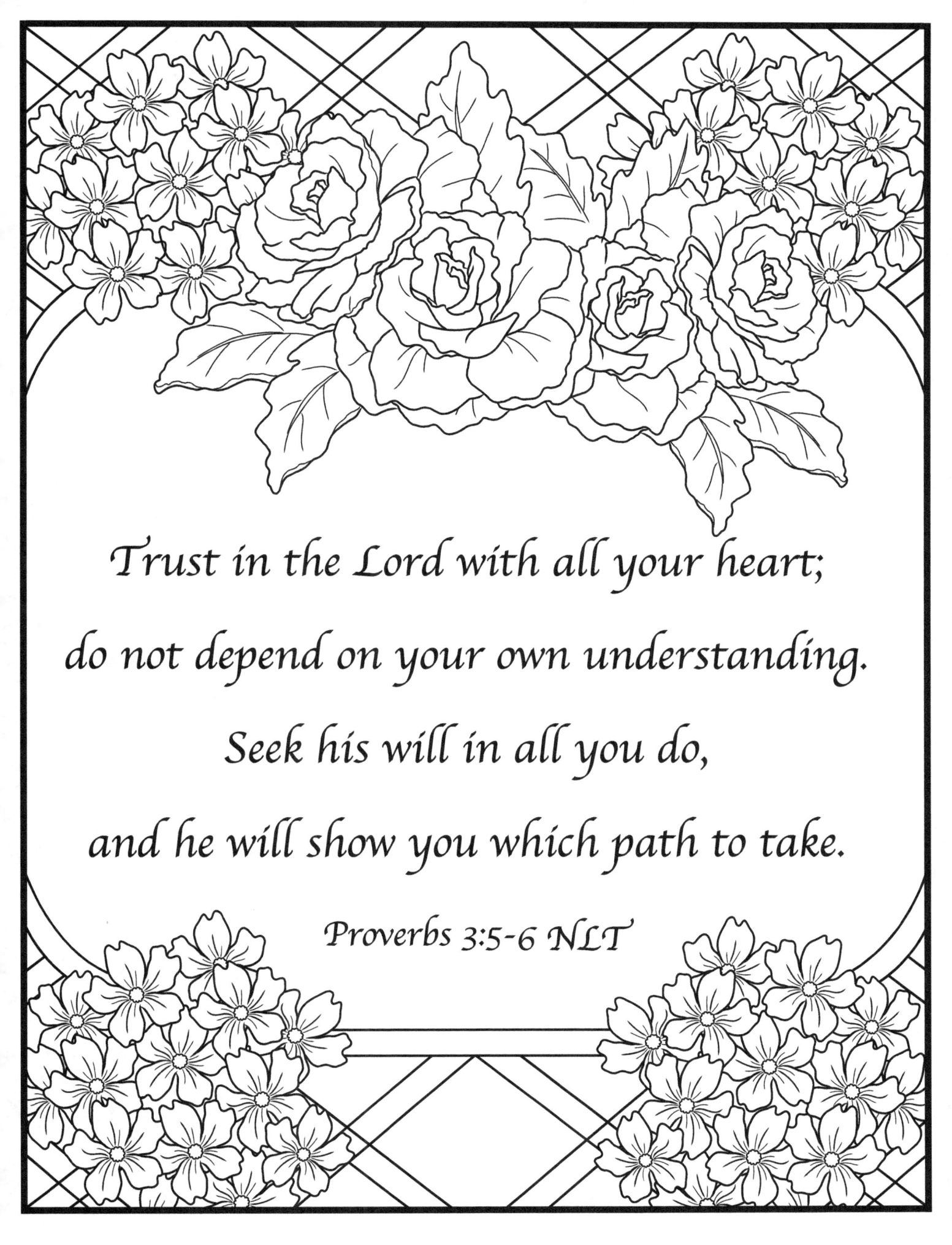

Trust in the Lord with all your heart;

do not depend on your own understanding.

Seek his will in all you do,

and he will show you which path to take.

Proverbs 3:5-6 NLT

Trust in God, He will direct your path.

Don't be afraid, for I am with you. Don't be discouraged, for I am your God. I will strengthen you and help you. I will hold you up with my victorious right hand.

Isaiah 41:10 NLT

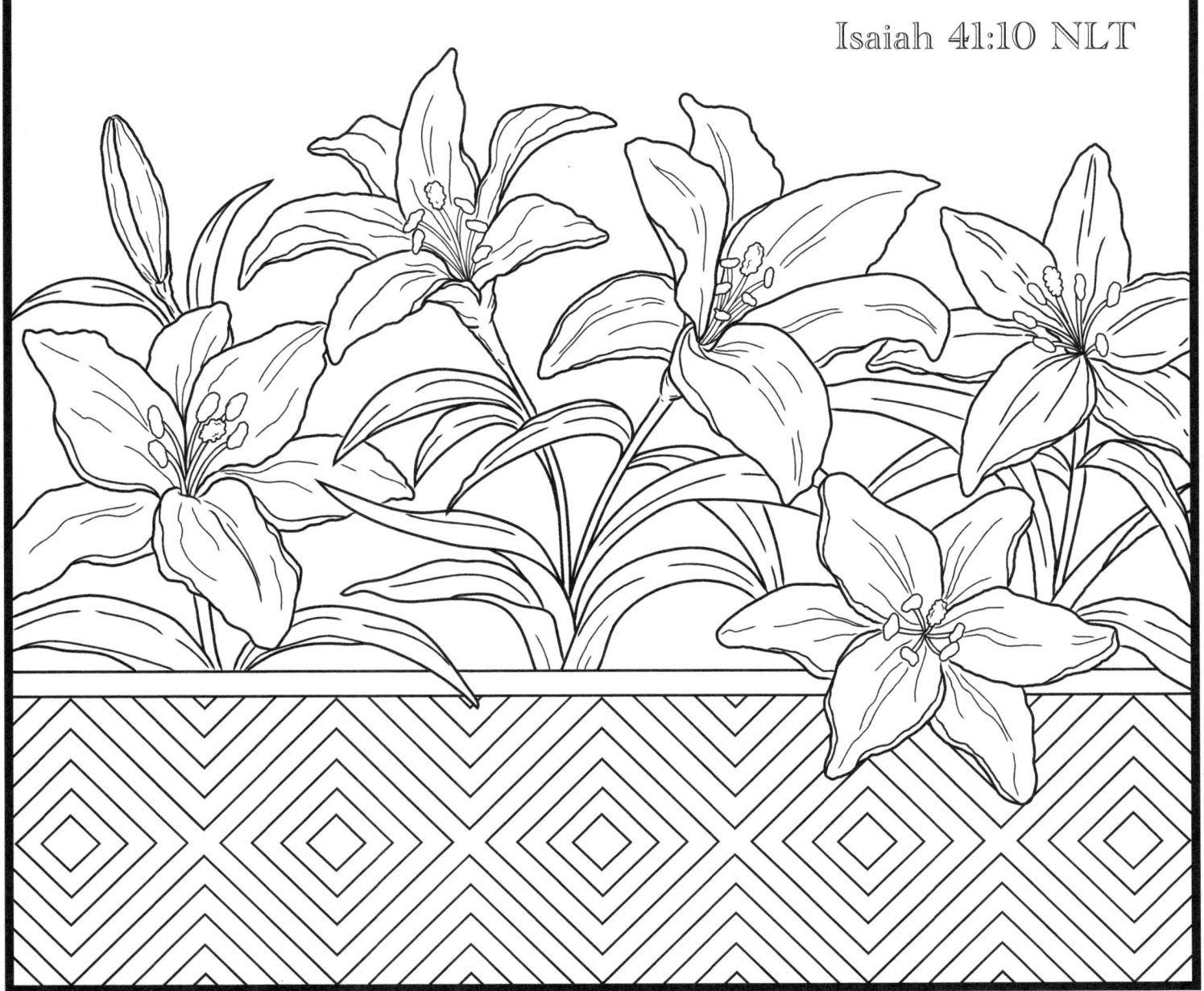

Trust in God, He will uphold you with His right hand.

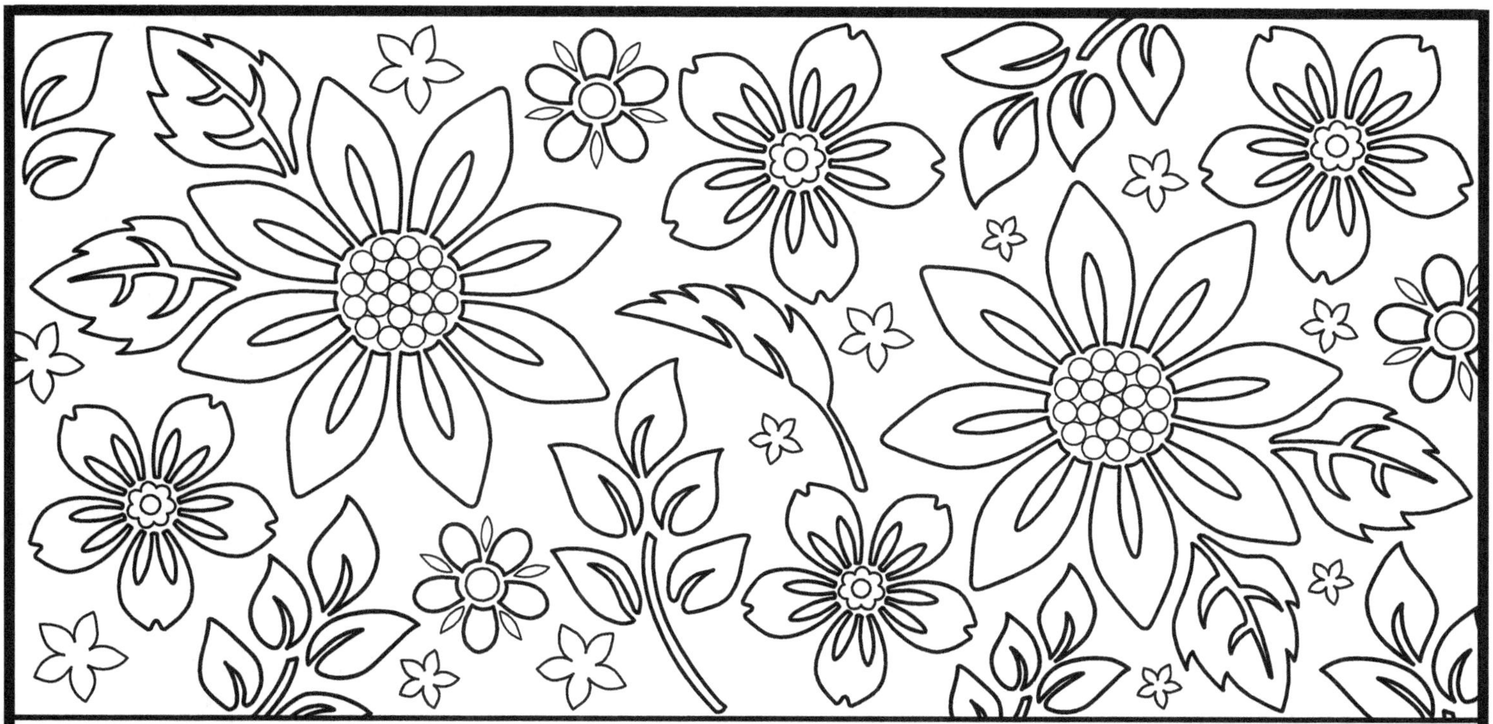

Give your burdens to the Lord, and he will take care of you. He will not permit the godly to slip and fall.

Psalm 55:22 NLT

Trust in God, He will lift your burdens.

May the God of hope fill you with all joy and peace as you trust in him, so that you may overflow with hope by the power of the Holy Spirit.

Romans 15:13 NIV

Trust in God, He will give you power by His Spirit.

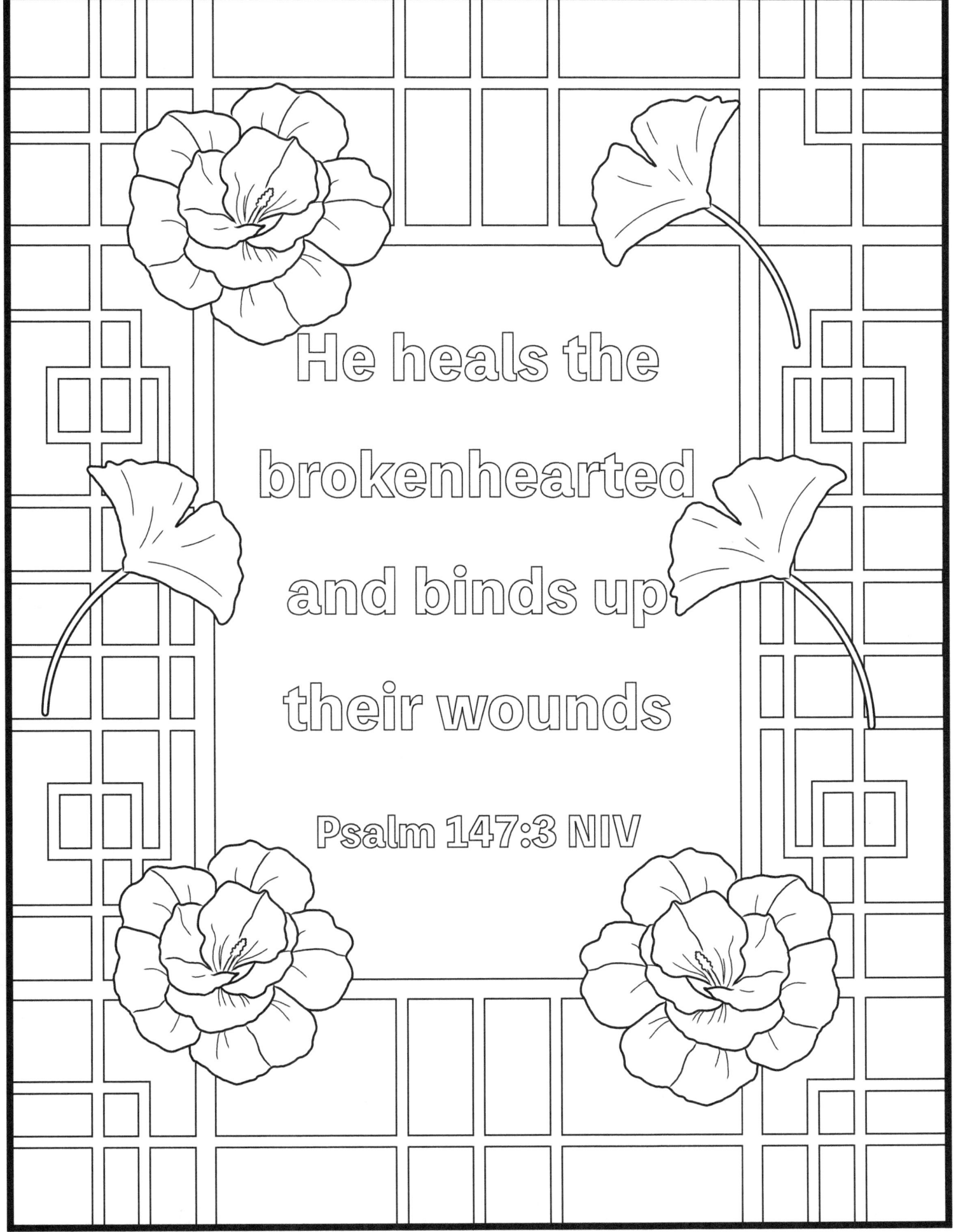

He heals the brokenhearted and binds up their wounds

Psalm 147:3 NIV

Trust in God, and He will heal your broken heart.

"Have I not commanded you? Be strong and courageous. Do not be afraid; do not be discouraged, for the LORD your God will be with you wherever you go."

Joshua 1:9 NIV

Trust in God, He will be with you wherever you go.

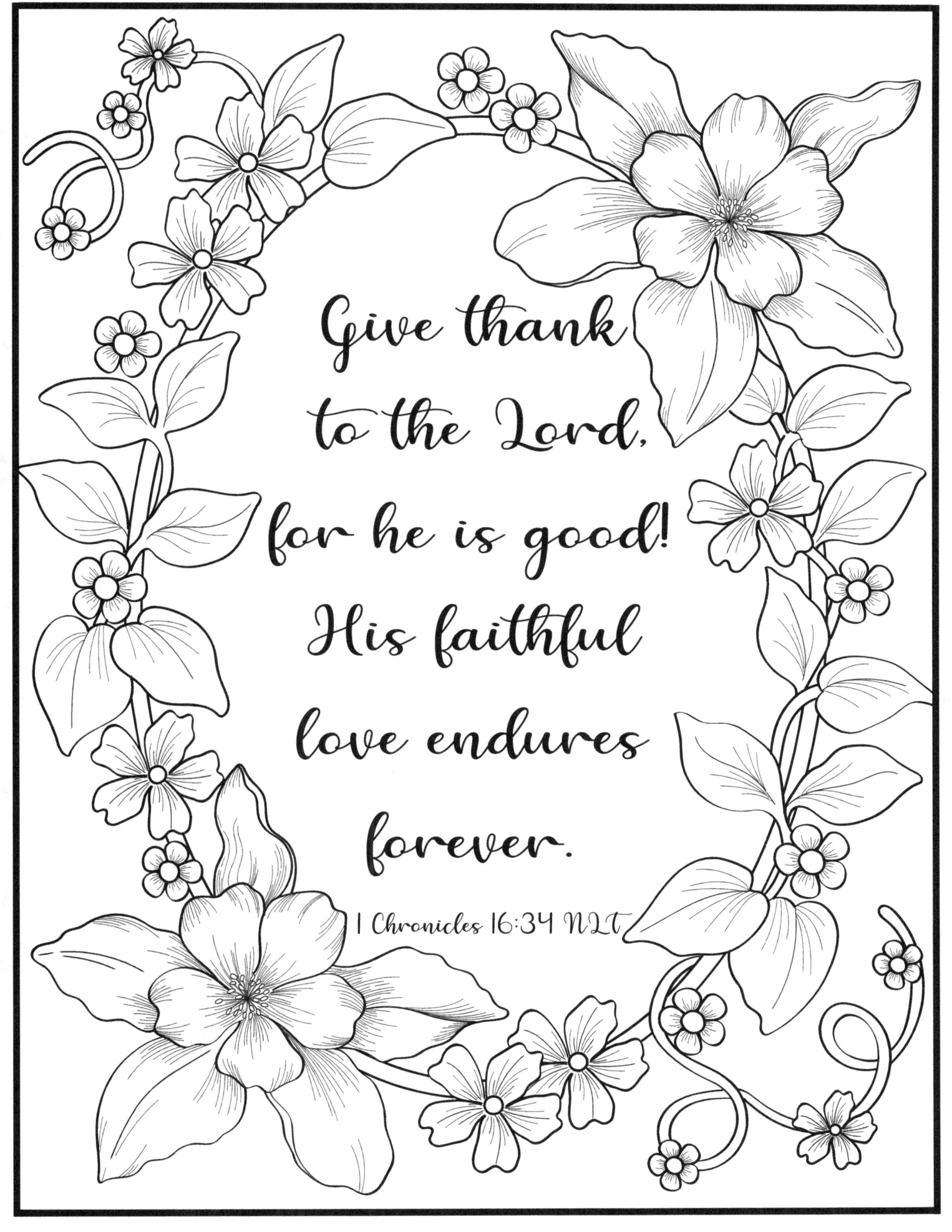

Trust in God, His faithful love endures forever.

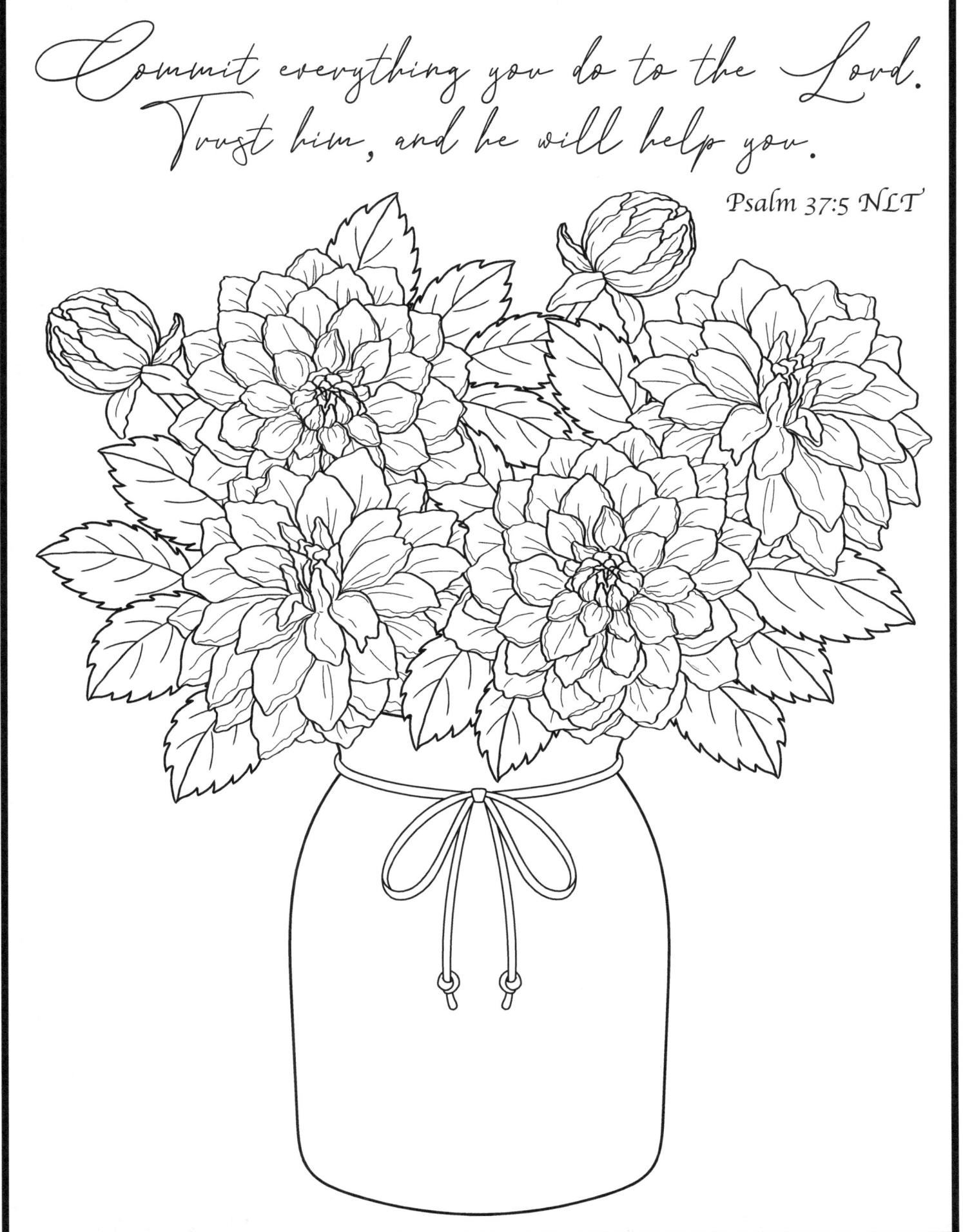

Trust in God and commit your life to Him.

The Lord hears his people when they call to him for help. He rescues them from all their troubles. The Lord is close to the brokenhearted; he rescues those whose spirits are crushed.

Psalm 34:17-18 NLT

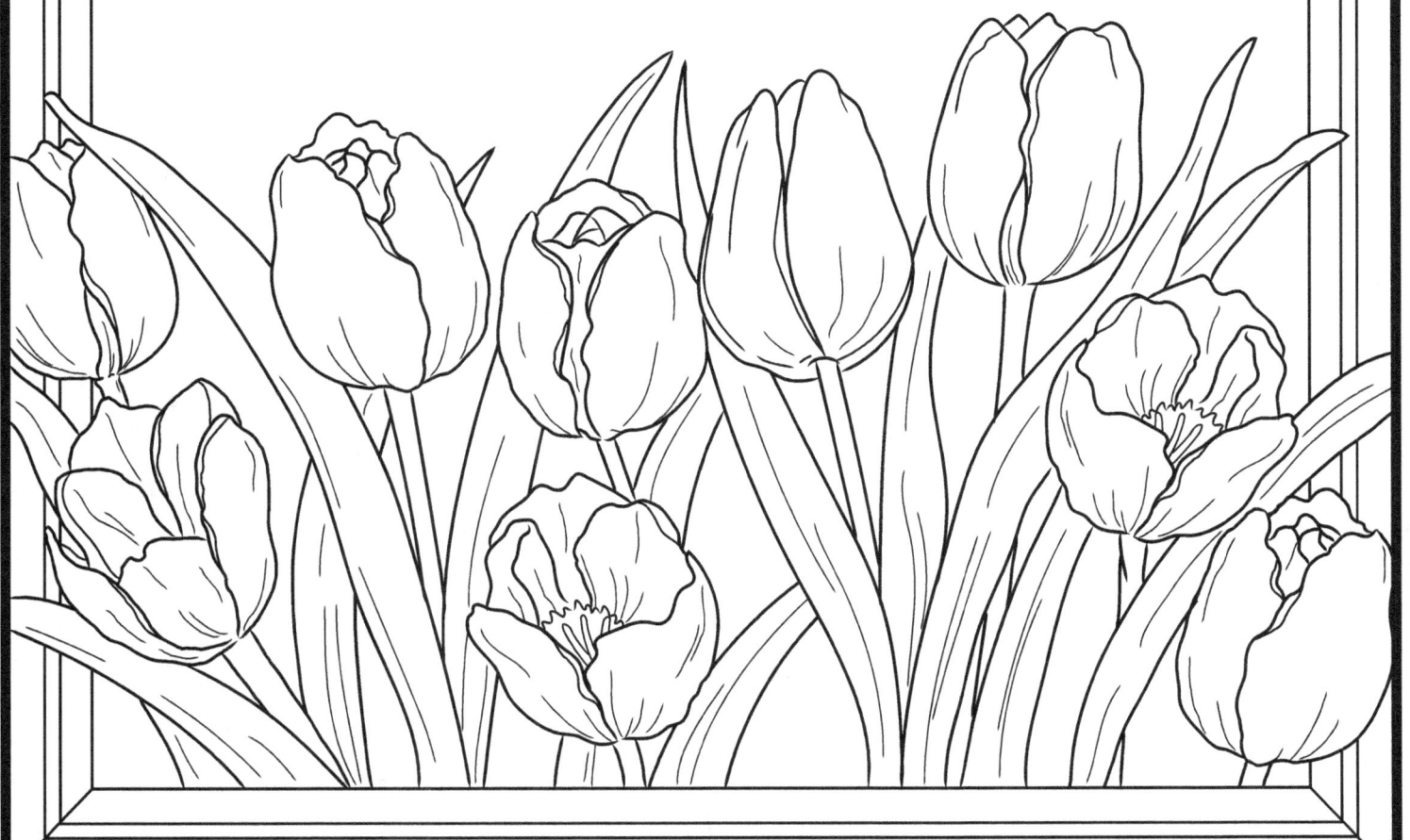

Trust in God, He will rescue you.

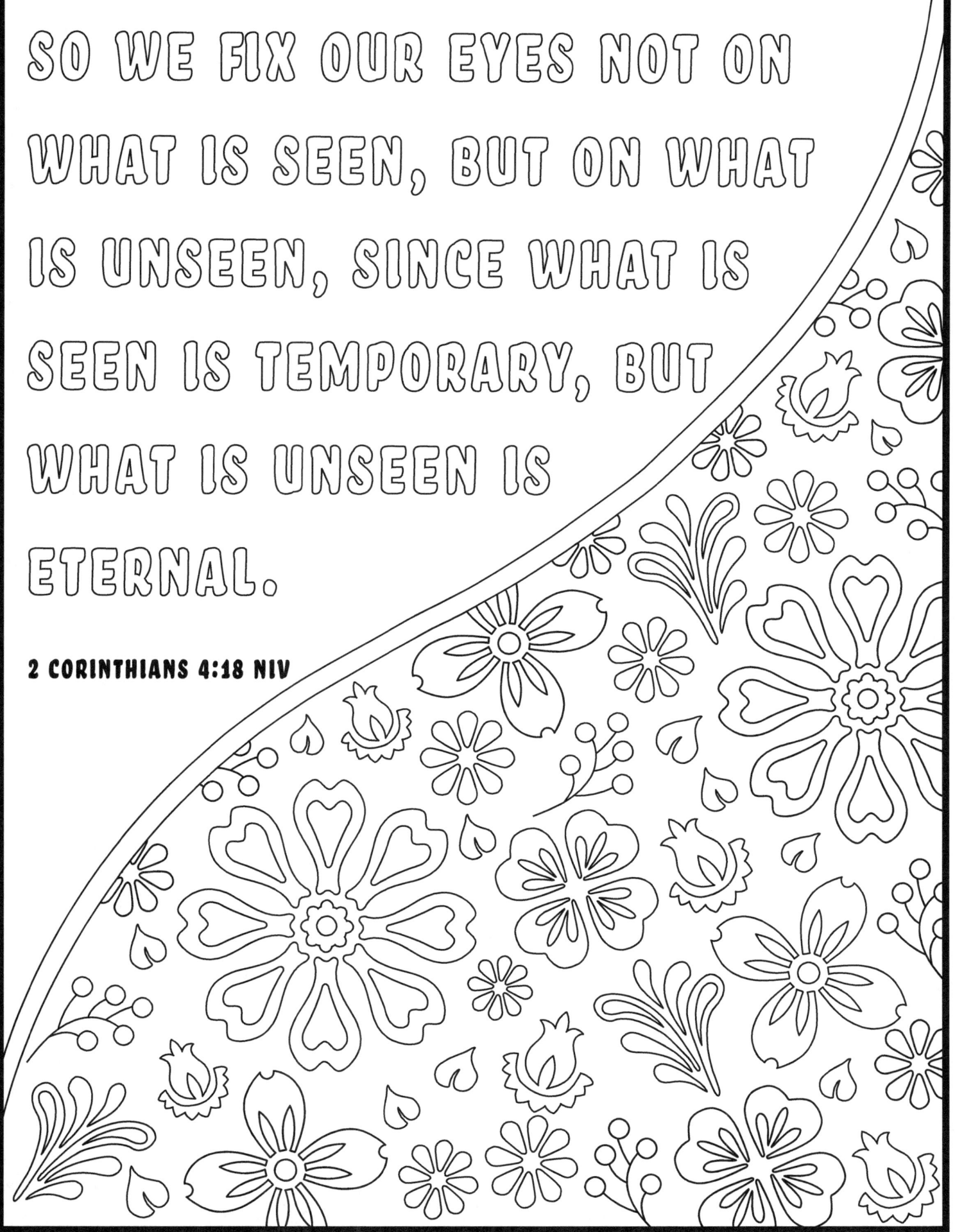

SO WE FIX OUR EYES NOT ON WHAT IS SEEN, BUT ON WHAT IS UNSEEN, SINCE WHAT IS SEEN IS TEMPORARY, BUT WHAT IS UNSEEN IS ETERNAL.

2 CORINTHIANS 4:18 NIV

Trust in God, and fix your eyes on Him.

Give all your worries and cares to God, for he cares about you.

1 Peter 5:7 NLT

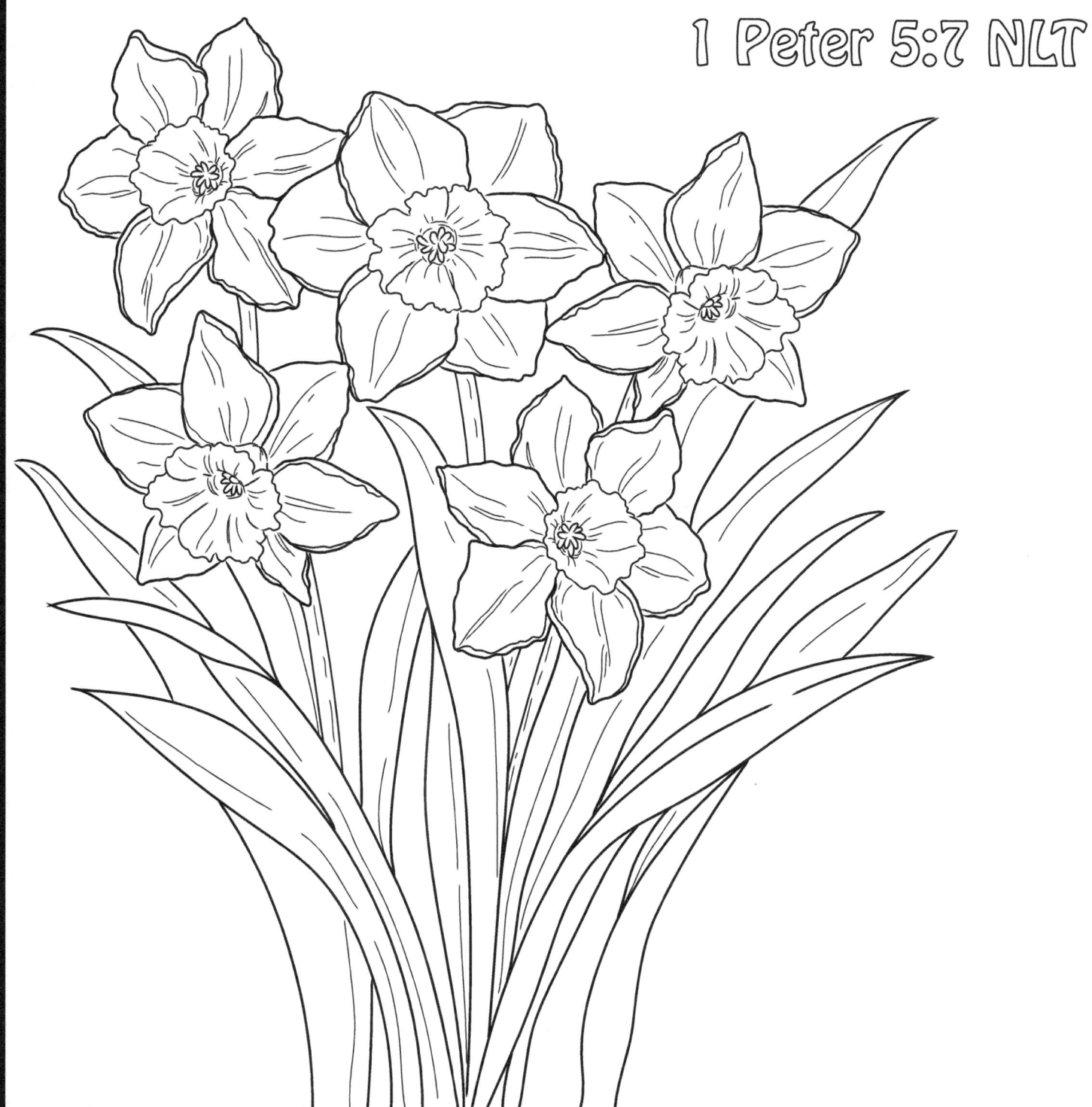

Trust in God for He cares for you.

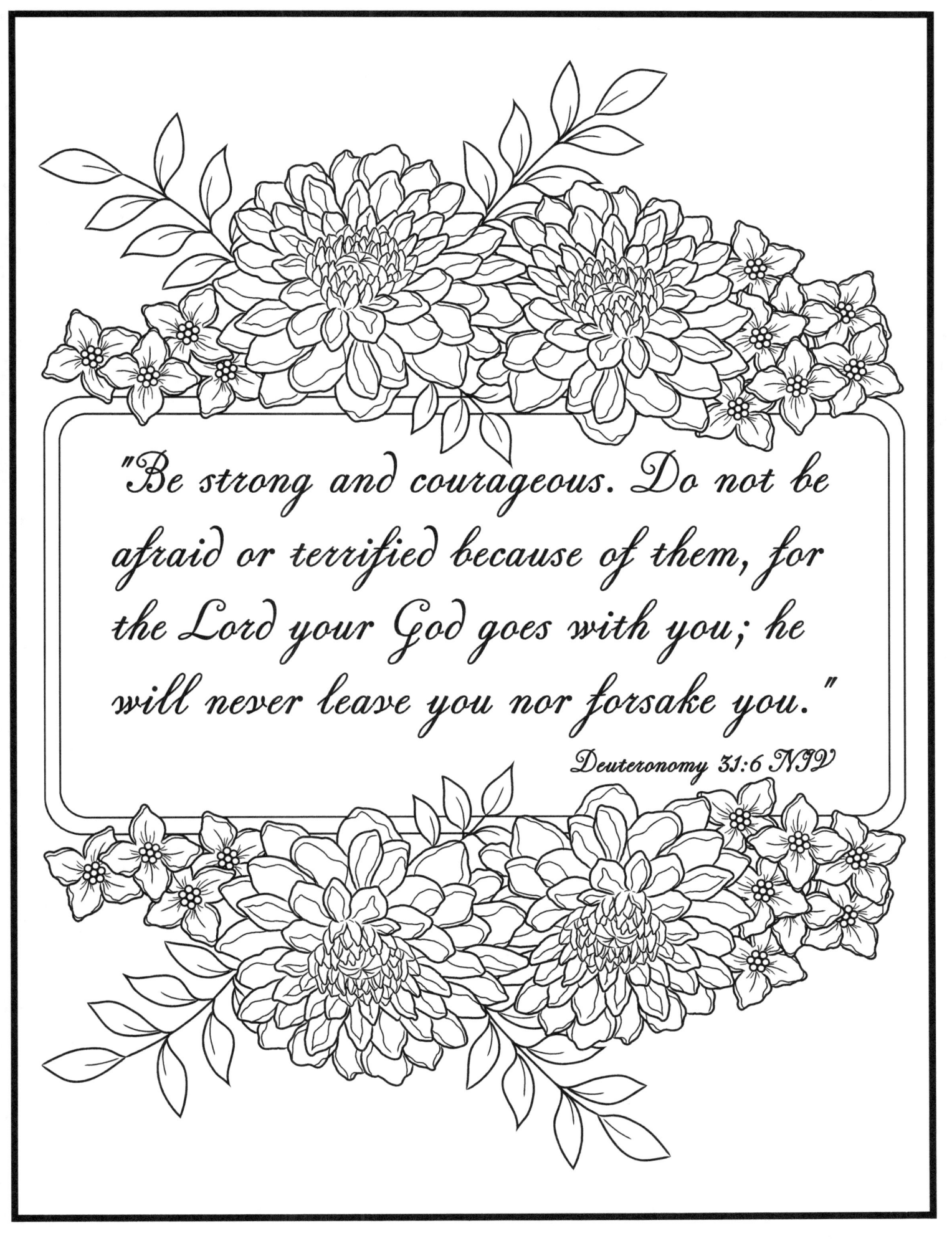

Trust in God, He will never leave or forsake you.

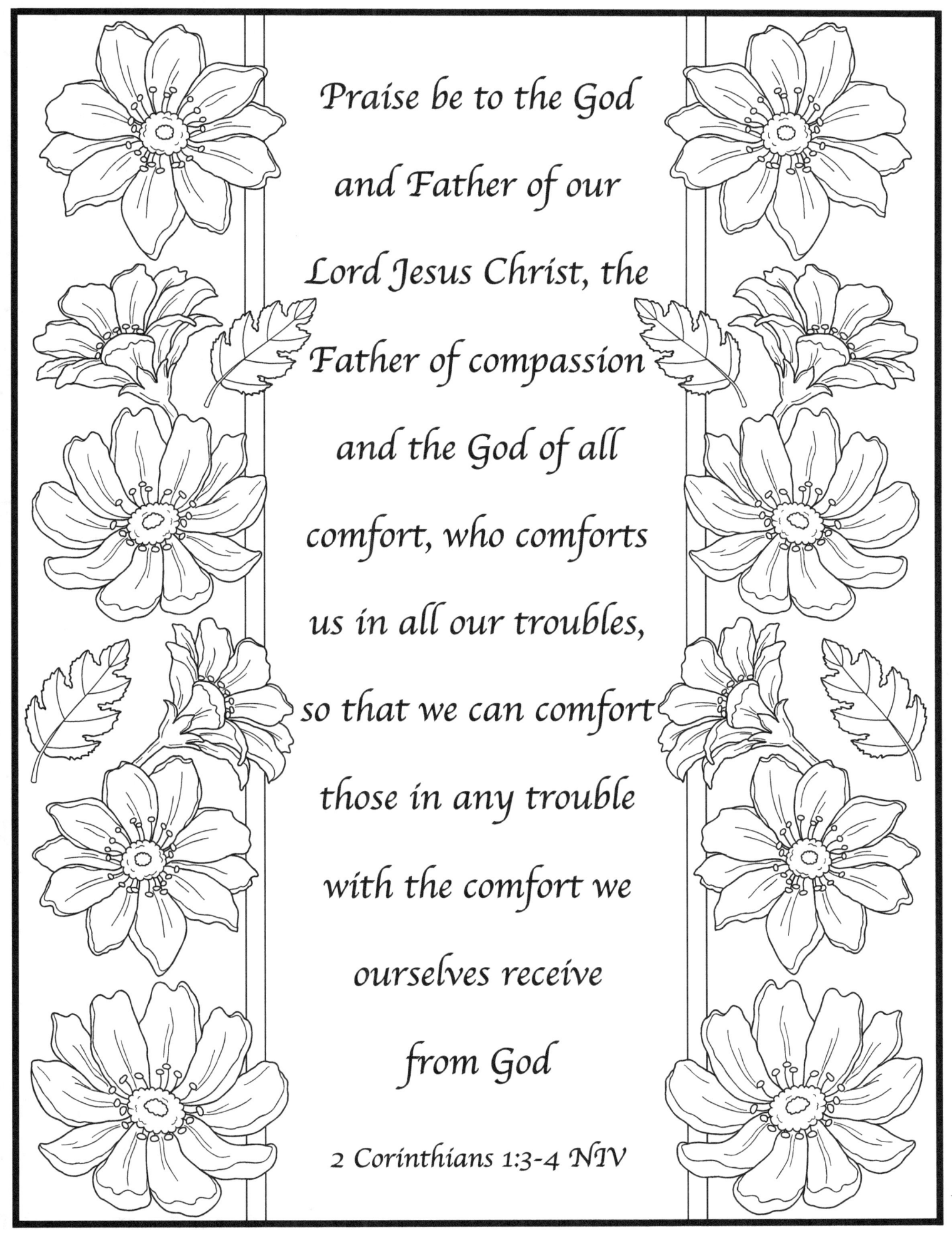

Praise be to the God
and Father of our
Lord Jesus Christ, the
Father of compassion
and the God of all
comfort, who comforts
us in all our troubles,
so that we can comfort
those in any trouble
with the comfort we
ourselves receive
from God

2 Corinthians 1:3-4 NIV

Trust in God for He is the God of all comfort.

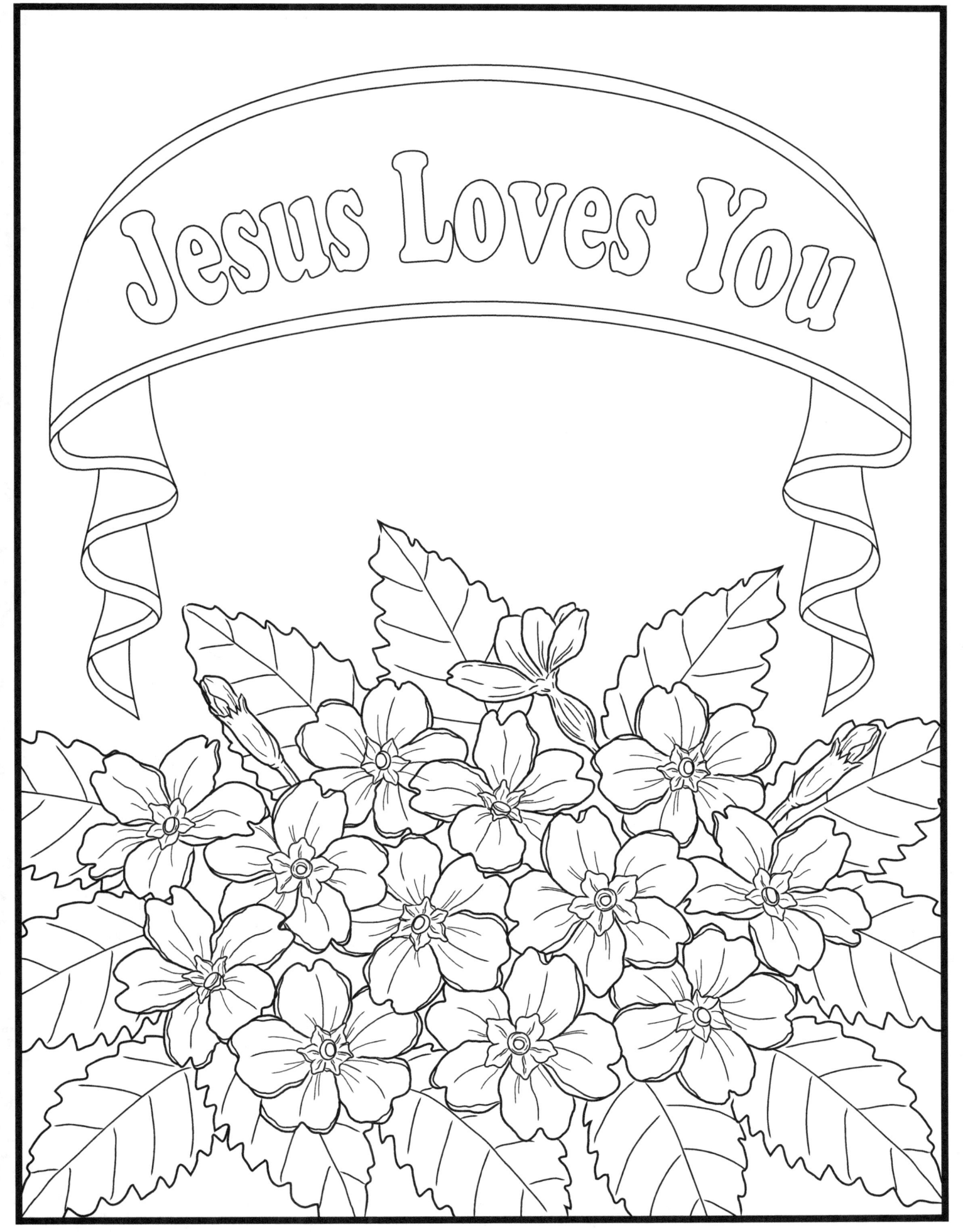

Trust in God for He loves you.

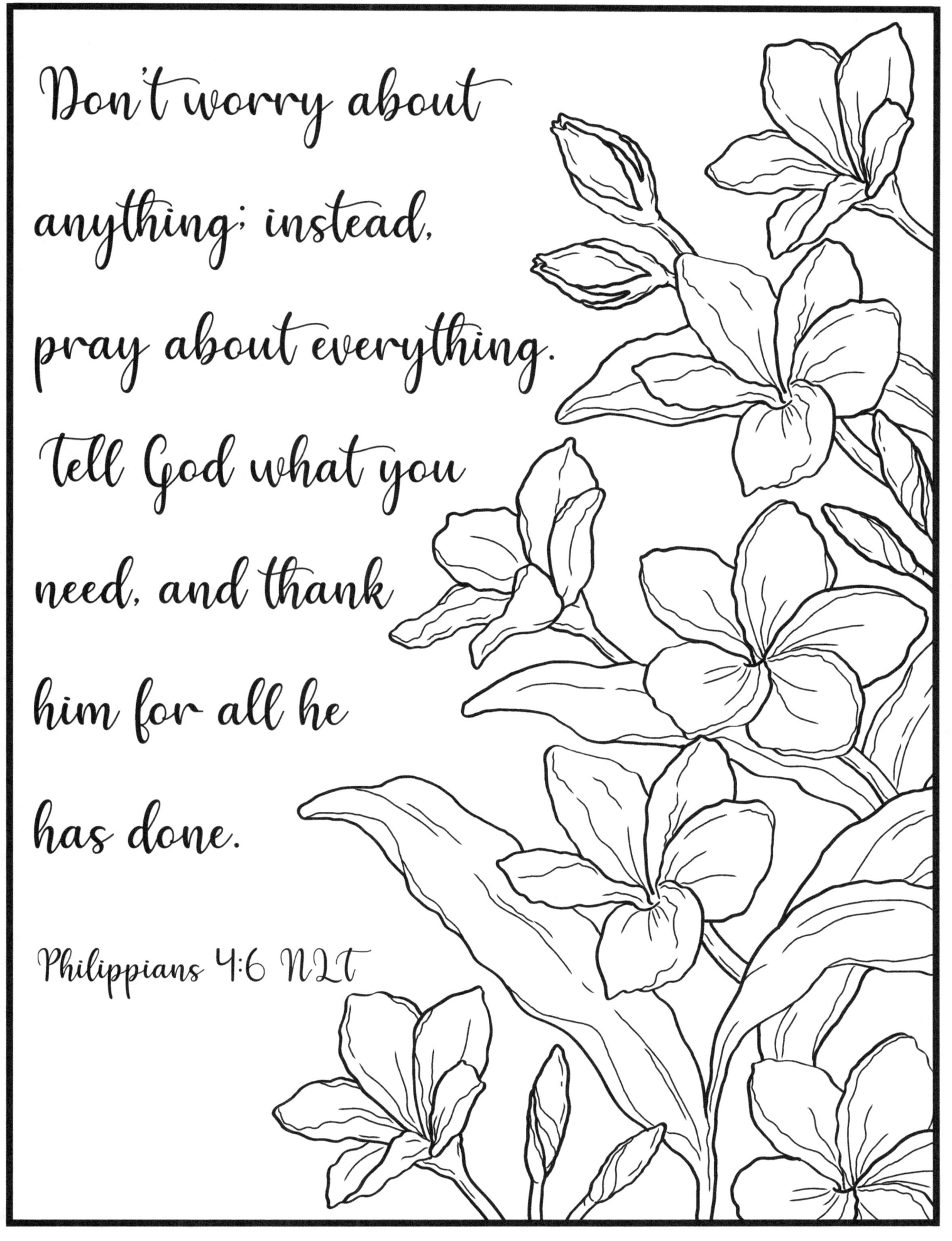

Don't worry about anything; instead, pray about everything. Tell God what you need, and thank him for all he has done.

Philippians 4:6 NLT

Trust in God and do not be anxious.

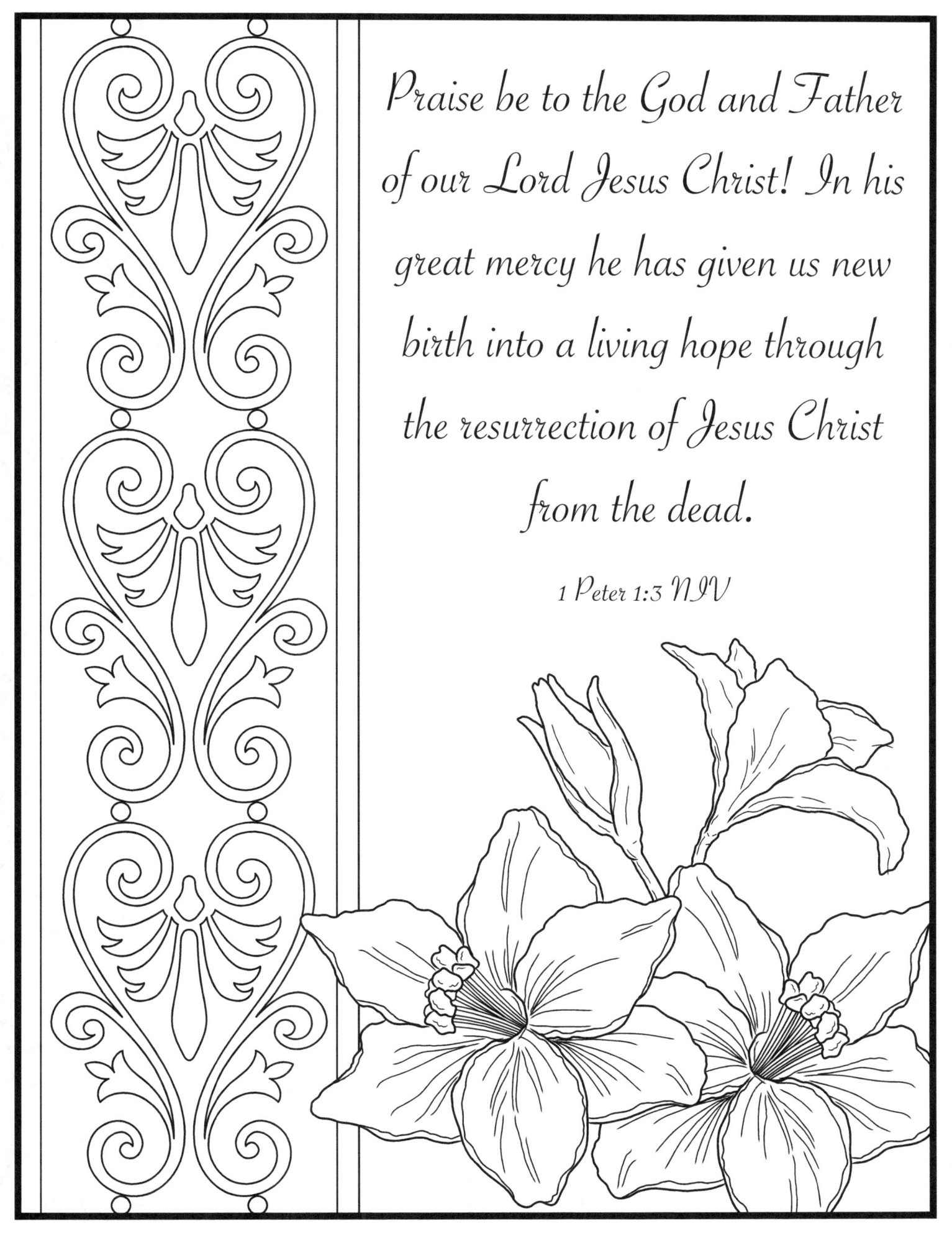

Praise be to the God and Father of our Lord Jesus Christ! In his great mercy he has given us new birth into a living hope through the resurrection of Jesus Christ from the dead.

1 Peter 1:3 NIV

Trust in God for He is our living hope.

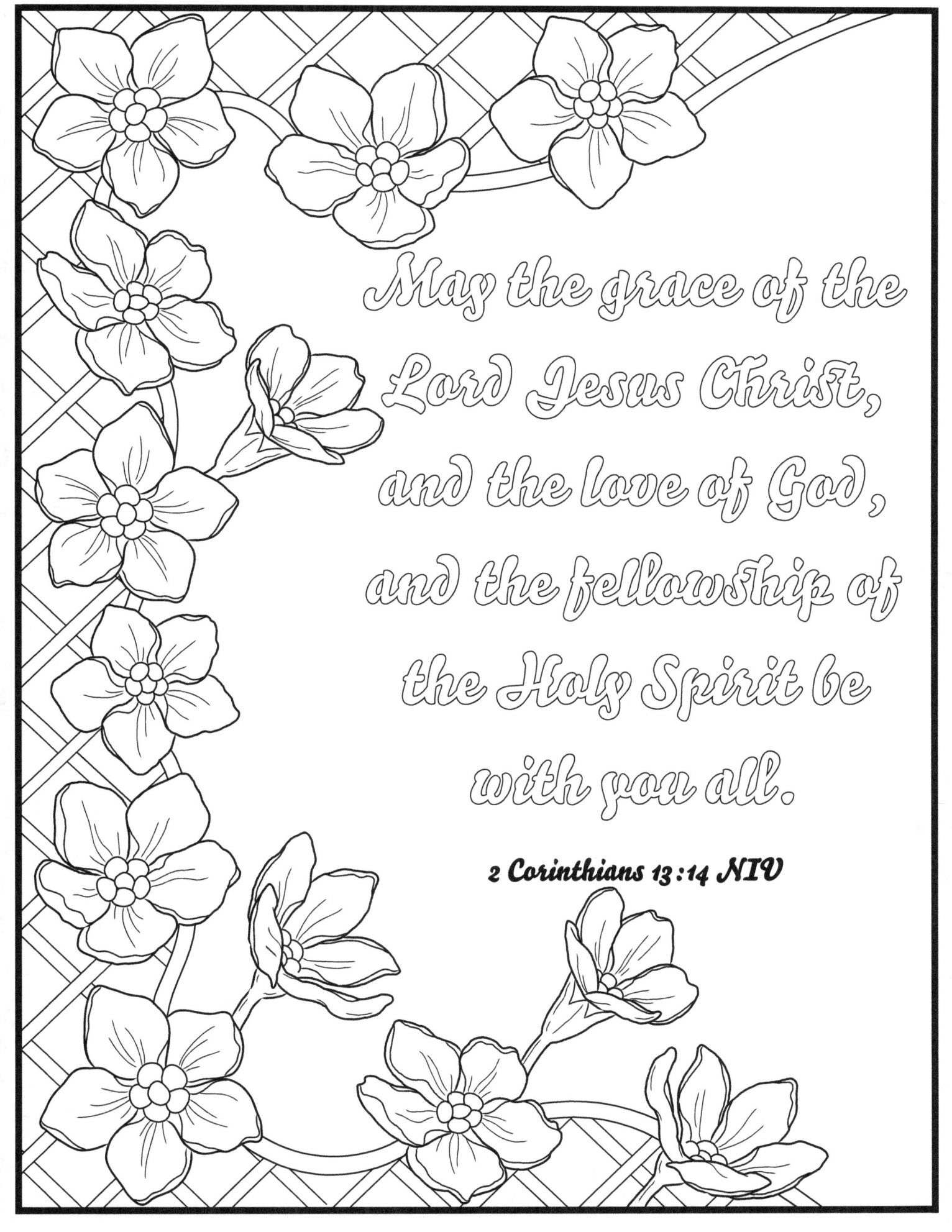

May the grace of the Lord Jesus Christ, and the love of God, and the fellowship of the Holy Spirit be with you all.

2 Corinthians 13:14 NIV

Trust in God for His grace and love covers you.

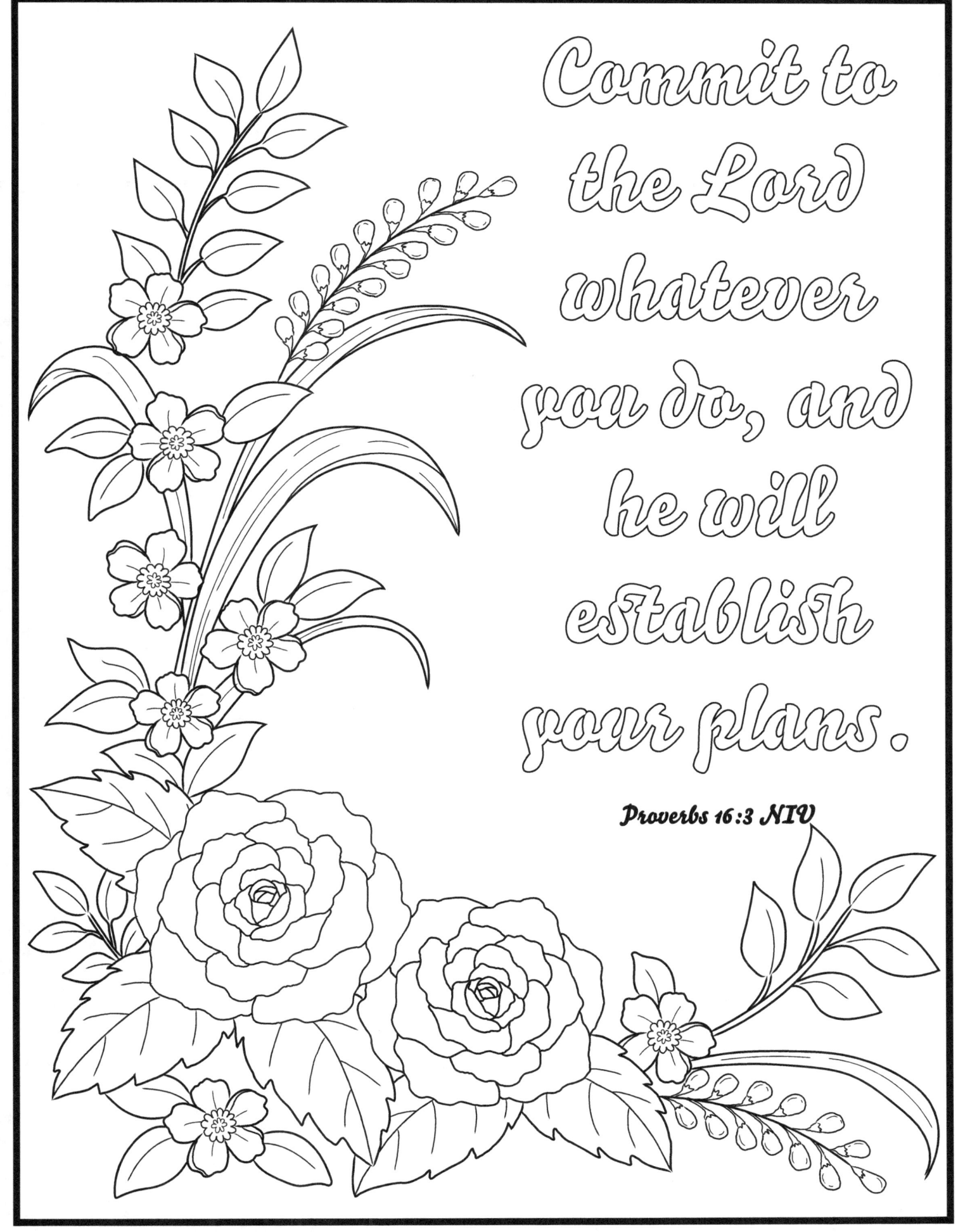

Commit to the Lord whatever you do, and he will establish your plans.

Proverbs 16:3 NIV

Trust in God in whatever you do.

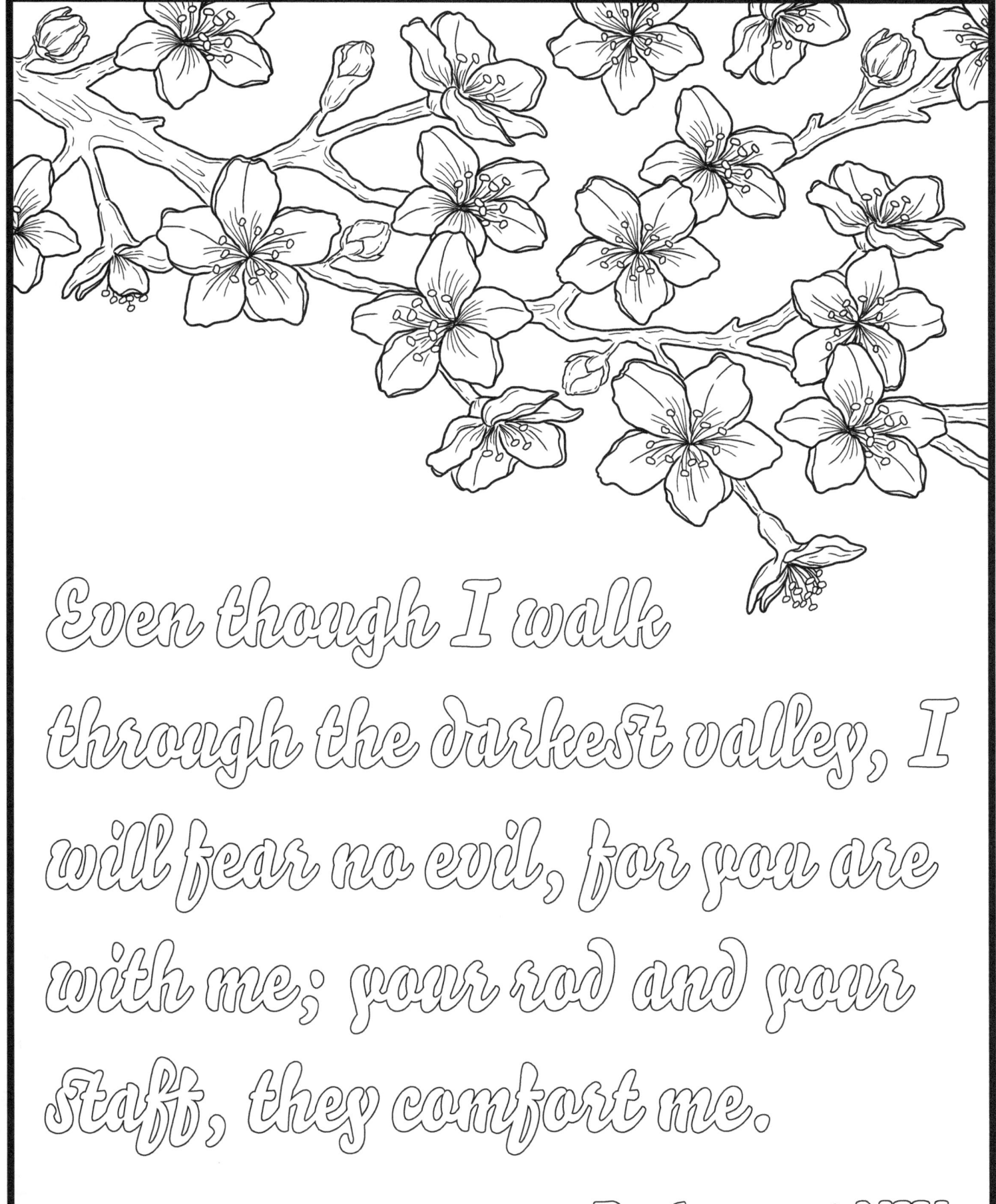

Even though I walk through the darkest valley, I will fear no evil, for you are with me; your rod and your staff, they comfort me.

Psalm 23:4 NIV

Trust in God in all situations.

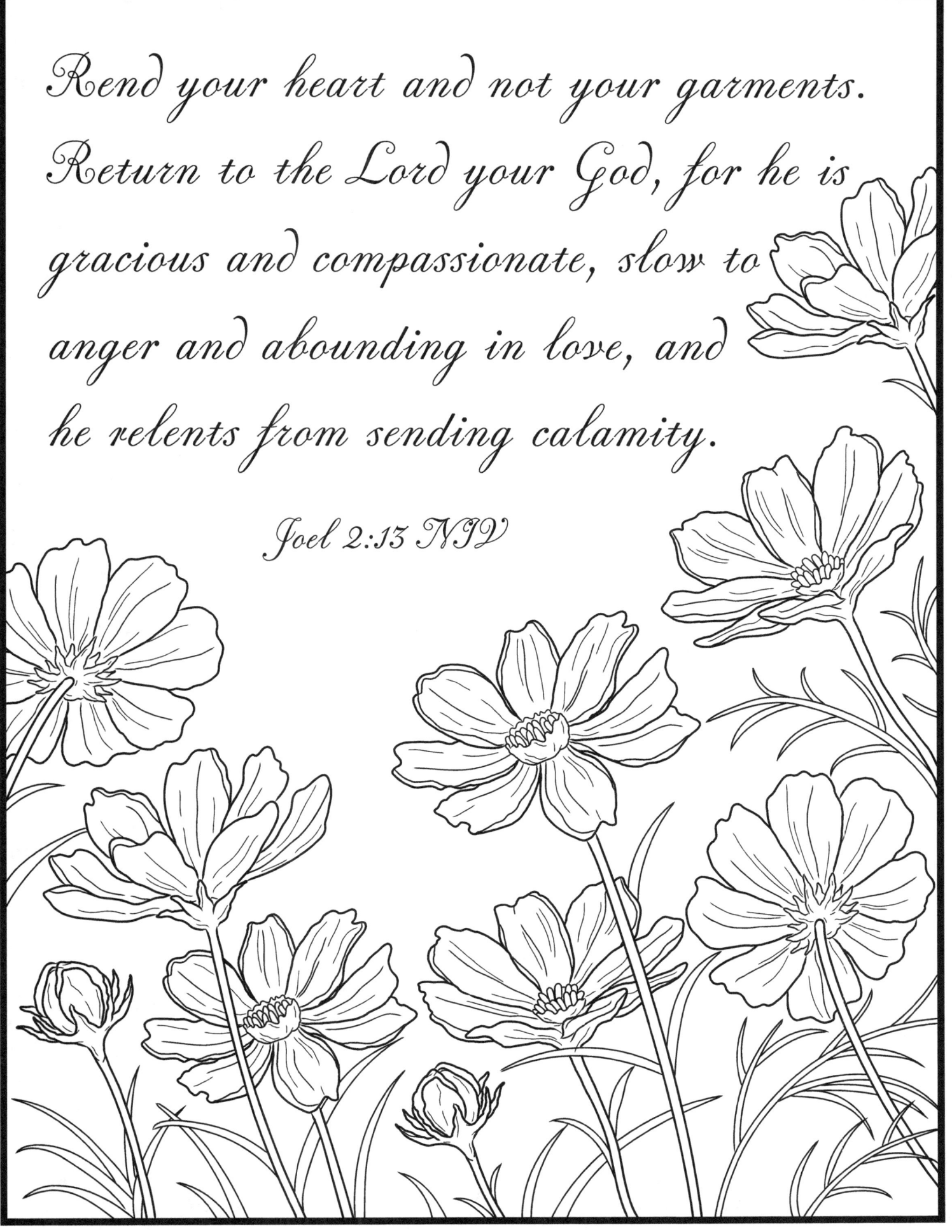

Rend your heart and not your garments.
Return to the Lord your God, for he is
gracious and compassionate, slow to
anger and abounding in love, and
he relents from sending calamity.

Joel 2:13 NIV

Trust in God, for He is a gracious and compassionate God.

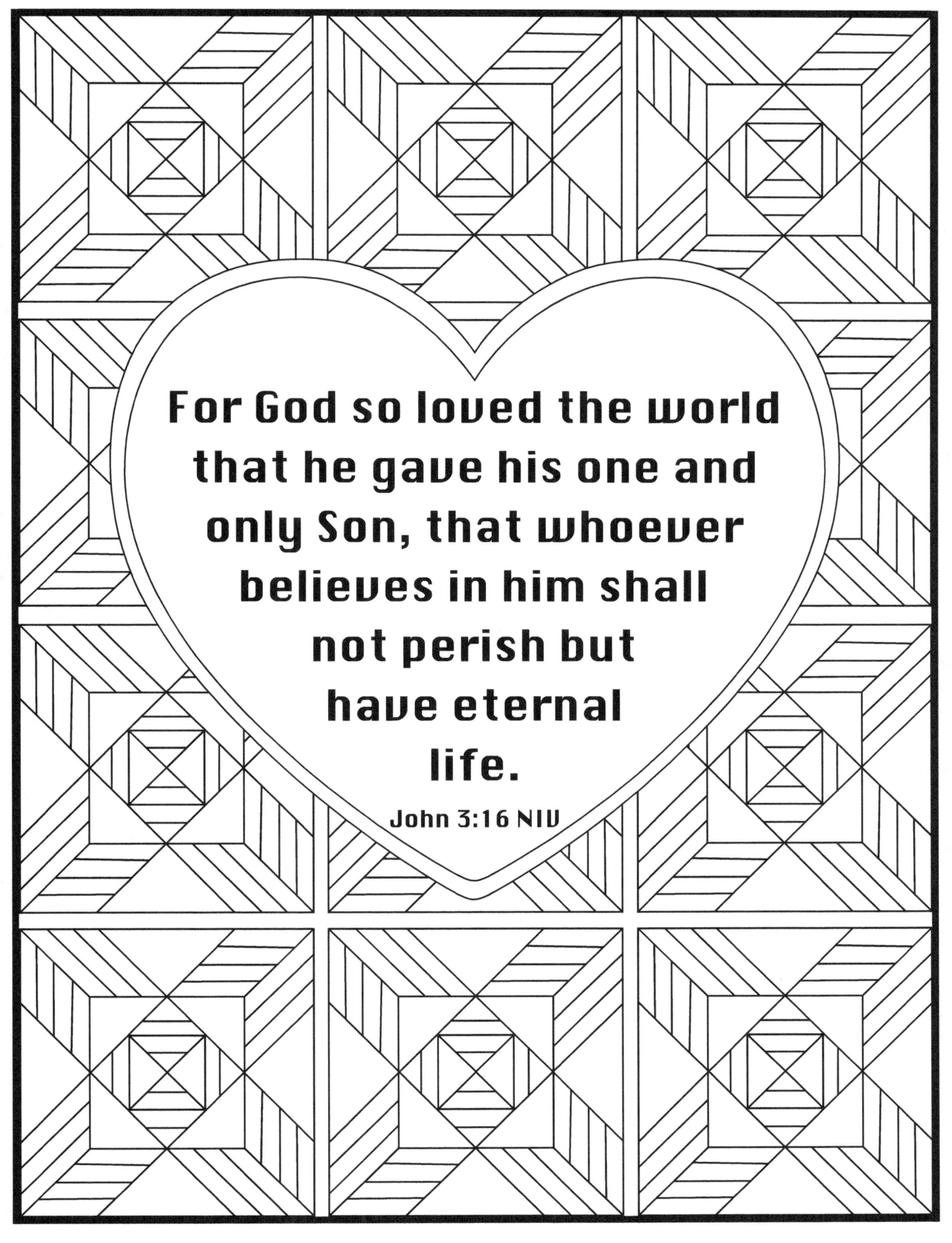

For God so loved the world that he gave his one and only Son, that whoever believes in him shall not perish but have eternal life.

John 3:16 NIV

Trust in God, and you will have eternal life.

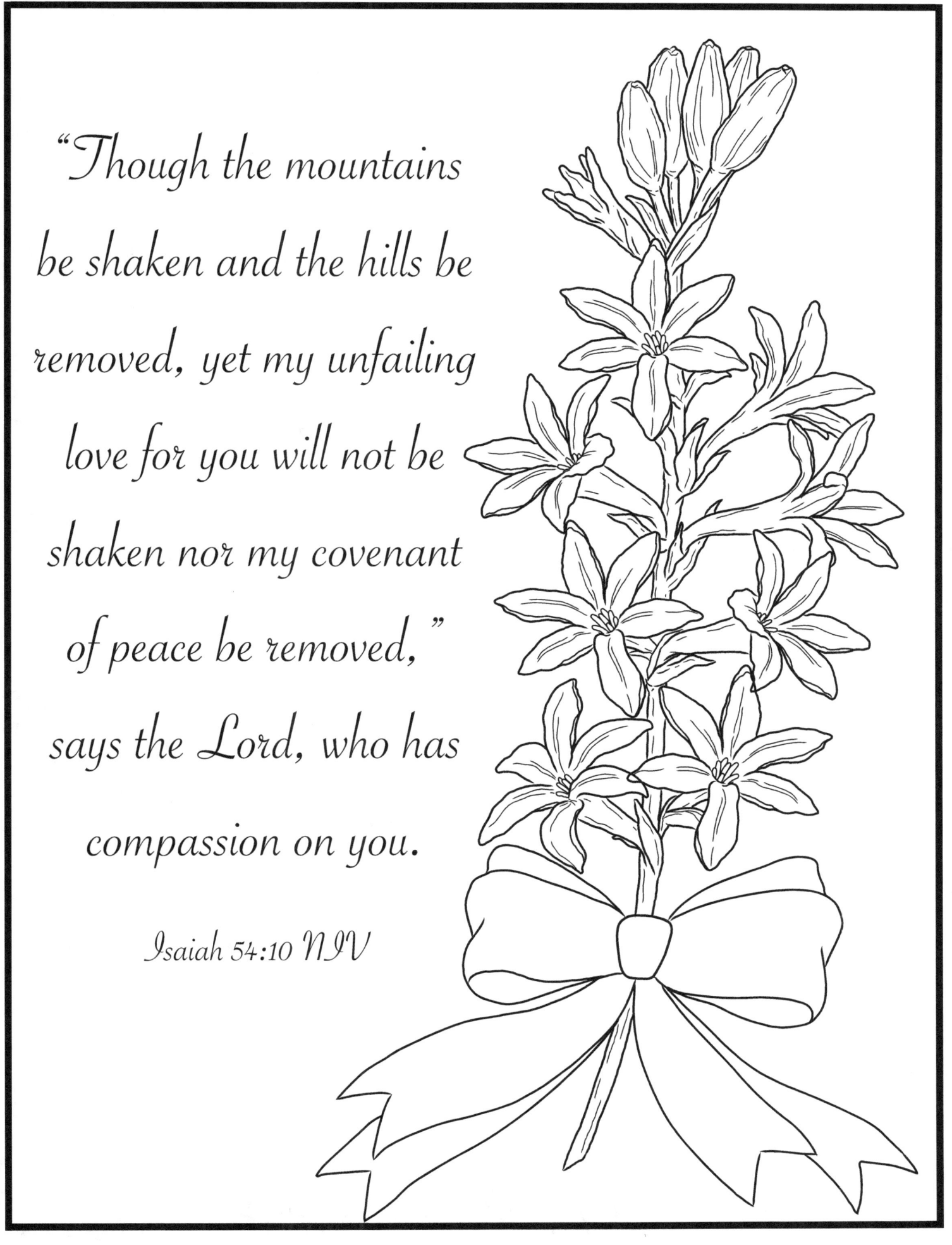

"Though the mountains be shaken and the hills be removed, yet my unfailing love for you will not be shaken nor my covenant of peace be removed," says the Lord, who has compassion on you.

Isaiah 54:10 NIV

Trust in God, He is your foundation.

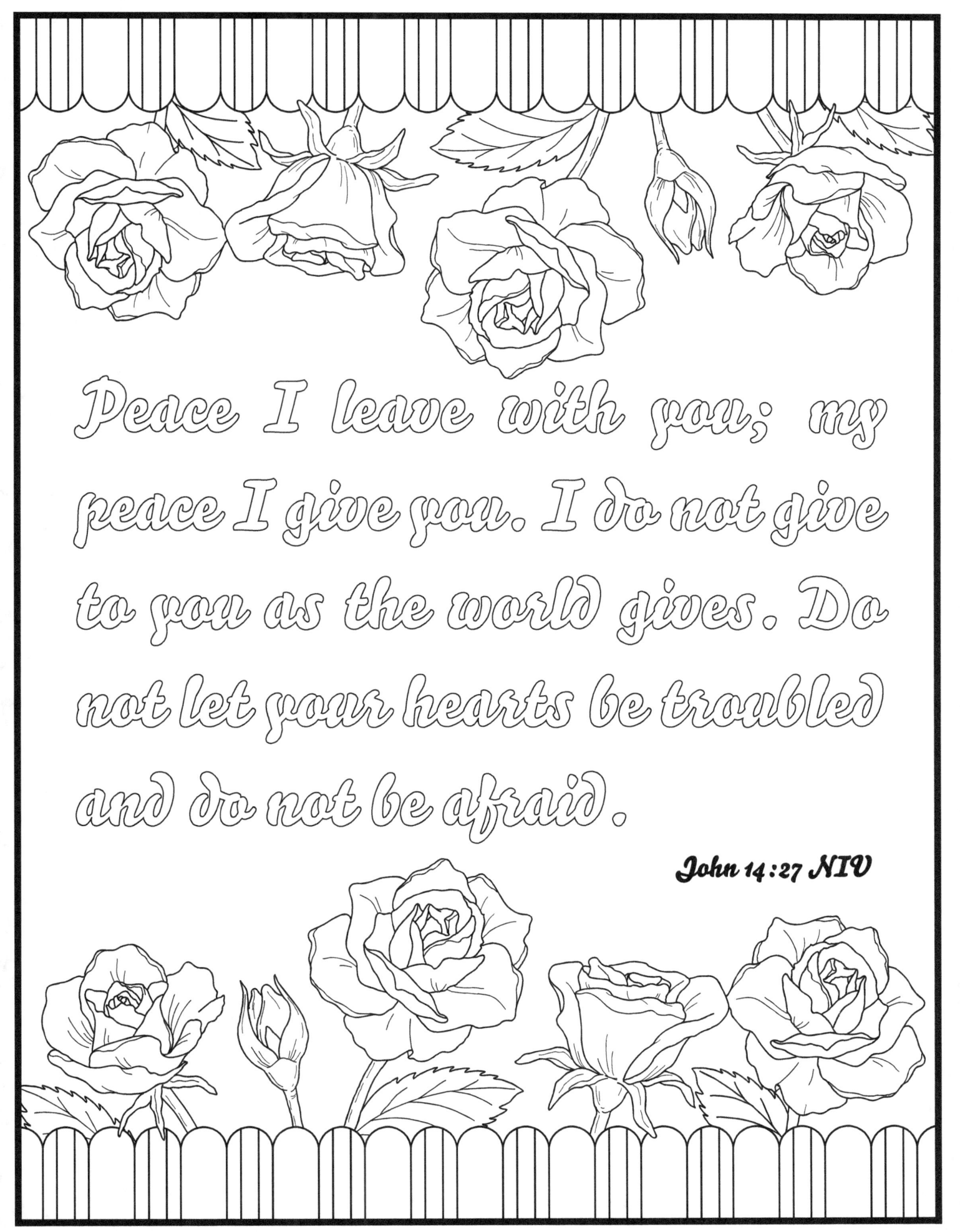

Trust in God, He is your peace.

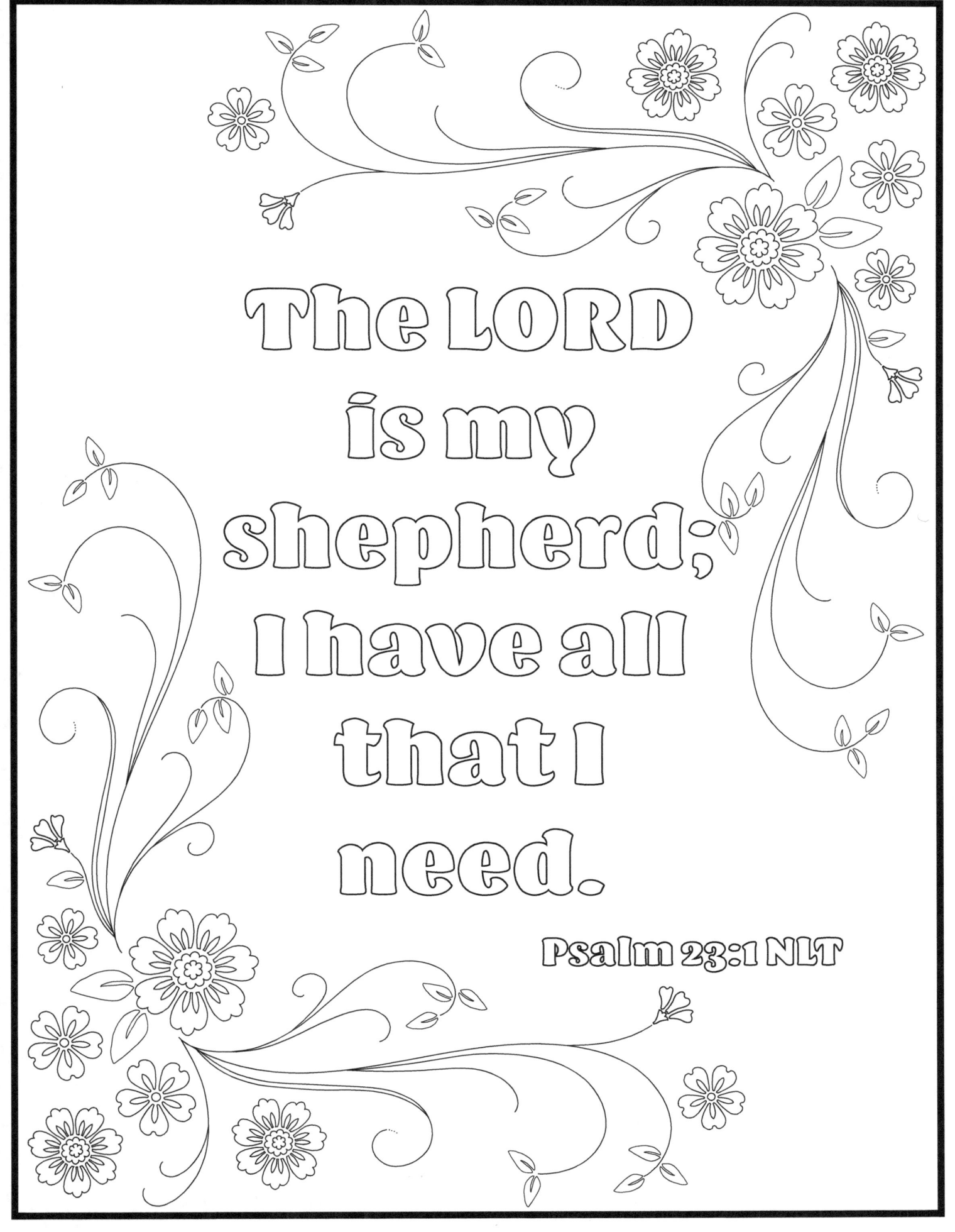

Trust in God, He will give you all that you need.